# Grandma

# Joy's

## Hope for Hurting Women

To Billie,

Bless you!

Love,

Grandma Joy Whittaker

919 736-4408

DESTINY IMAGE® PUBLISHERS, INC.
P.O. Box 310, Shippensburg, PA 17257-0310

"*Speaking to the Purposes of God for this Generation
and for the Generations to Come.*"

This book and all other Destiny Image, Revival Press, MercyPlace, Fresh Bread, Destiny Image Fiction, and Treasure House books are available at Christian bookstores and distributors worldwide.

' For a U.S. bookstore nearest you, call 1-800-722-6774.
For more information on foreign distributors, call 717-532-3040.

Or reach us on the Internet:
**www.destinyimage.com**

ISBN 10: 0-7684-2351-1
ISBN 13: 978-0-7684-2351-8

For Worldwide Distribution, Printed in the U.S.A.

1 2 3 4 5 6 7 8 9 10 11 / 09 08 07 06

# Dedication

This book is lovingly dedicated to all my family and friends, especially my parents, grandmother, and my son, Troy, for their generous support and unconditional love.

May God continue to bless you all as you walk with His divine purpose.

# Acknowledgements

I acknowledge gratitude to the instructors and professors at Wayne Community College in Goldsboro, North Carolina; East Carolina University in Greenville, North Carolina; and, Wesleyan College, Goldsboro, North Carolina. I appreciate the dedication and kindness you've shown me throughout the years. Thank you for publishing my short stories and for giving me an opportunity to create and perform. With my love for literature and theater and your instruction and guidance, I am able to spread my wings and fly.

I am also eternally grateful for all the love and support from members and friends at Saint Luke United Holy Church in Rose Hill, North Carolina. May God continue to bless you, all!

# Table of Contents

Preface ....................................................................................11

Introduction.........................................................................13

## SECTION I

### TRIBULATIONS & TESTIMONIES

The Stuff Inside My Old Couch ............................................17

Dear Lord ............................................................................31

I Am an Alcoholic................................................................33

The Blood of Jesus ...............................................................39

I Can't Get AIDS ................................................................41

A Wife's Promise .................................................................45

The Bag Lady.......................................................................47

Eagles in a Storm .................................................................51

Extreme Wedding Shower .....................................53

I Cannot Kill My Baby! ......................................55

Taking It Back.................................................59

Greener Grass ................................................67

In Love With a Married Man ...............................69

Little Johnny Tells All........................................79

Platonic Relationship .......................................81

Shortening Bread ...........................................83

Sitting In the Back Row of the Church.....................87

Mother's Day .................................................93

Footprints in the Snow ......................................93

Why?..........................................................95

The Faithful Church Member ...............................97

Worth a Penny ...............................................99

Woman in the Mirror.......................................101

Things Are Rarely Like They Seem .......................103

Succeed!.....................................................107

When He Leaves.............................................111

The Appointment ...........................................115

The Stubborn Mule ........................................117

God's Plan...................................................119

Don't Mess With Grandma! ...............................121

A Good Man Is Hard to Find .............................123

With God, All Things Are Possible! ......................127

My Husband's Secret .......................................131

Been Set Free................................................135

Just a Weeeee Bit.................................................139

A Time to Learn..................................................141

Don't You Know? ................................................143

I'm Sorry… .......................................................145

When I Say I'm Broke, I'm Broke.............................151

Forgiveness Is Necessary and Healing........................153

Two Little Mice...................................................155

My Sister's Keeper ..............................................157

The Outhouse.....................................................161

Extreme Makeover ..............................................165

It Takes a Village ...............................................169

More Than Conquerors.........................................171

A Mother's Love.................................................173

Missing Out.......................................................175

America's Next Top Mom .....................................179

The Four Wives .................................................181

Desperate Housewives .........................................183

## SECTION II

### GREAT WOMEN OF THE BIBLE
### AND THEIR DIVINE PURPOSE

Who Touched Me?................................................189

Ruth.................................................................193

Esther...............................................................197

To Kiss His Feet .................................................201

Woman at the Well..............................................205

The Woman Taken in Adultery..............................209

From the Master's Table...................................211

## SECTION III

### YOUR TURN TO LIVE OUT
### YOUR DIVINE PURPOSE

Letter from God to Women .................................215

Your Purpose..............................................219

Prayer of Divine Purpose .................................223

Your Future ..............................................227

Conclusion ...............................................229

# Preface

As you read the stories in this book, try to look at the individuals through the eyes of God. You might easily empathize with the victim(s), and you may become angry with those who have been accused. However, please try to remember that condemnation comes easy. The world condemns! Sometimes, it is difficult to see God's divine purpose. After reading each story, ask yourself: What is God's divine destiny for the victim in this story?

# Introduction

## *Walking In Your Divine Destiny*

Oh great woman of God, it is your season for greatness! Even while you are in your "wilderness," you are not alone. God is with you and He has equipped you to "come out" victoriously!

This book is designed to help you realize that no matter what man says about you, God has given you a divine purpose; you have a divine destiny. This book will help you find your purpose and walk with a purpose, because without a purpose in God, your destiny cannot be complete.

You are still in your youthfulness: meaning, you haven't outlived your purpose. You haven't because if you had outlived your purpose, you would be dead. You're alive today for a reason. Remember that everything that God does...is "with purpose."

Your destiny is a place that your spirit already knows about and believes in, but your physical body has to catch up and realize your true divine position.

Your destiny is inside of you, and even your past pain (regardless of how tragic) will be a testimony for others, and many people will be saved through your testimony (through your past pain).

Some of you have been attacked, deeply scarred, and beaten up by the enemy. Please don't be bitter, but know that this is your "awakening season" and that the harvest is ready and plentiful.

God wants to restore (unto you) all the years that the locusts have eaten. Always remember that if "you don't go through anything," you "won't" have anything to tell anyone. Your victory rests on your testimony!

Say to all those who criticize you, "Don't look at me in my present state! But instead, look at me through the eyes of God!"

What you see today is temporary! Your present situation cannot dictate where you're "going" with God. Redemption has two parts, a "going in" and a "going out." You might have gone into a situation broke, busted, disgusted, and with a "just can't take it anymore" attitude. God wants to bring you out a winner!

*God wants to bring you to a flourishing finish.* When we have been abused and cheated, we're in a position to receive favor from God.

*I want you to know that you can be set free!* You may be filled with resentment, anger, depression, or with overwhelming guilt and shame. You might think that you are the only one suffering in the manner in which you are suffering, or that you are suffering because you are being punished by God; however, as you read this book, you will find that your sin isn't any greater than the sins of others.

Sin is sin, and God has a solution for sin. Jesus is the solution, and you will find helpful stories and testimonies about sin and suffering and God's solution to sin and pain in this book.

Oh great woman of God, continue to love Him in your prayers. As you read this book, know that God has been waiting for you and loving you since the beginning of time. God has a wonderful plan for your life! The door is open; the way has been made! There is going to be a "great move of God" like never before. Expect God's revelation and His glory over your life as you read this book. *It's time for you to live with a purpose and to walk into your divine destiny!*

# SECTION I

## Tribulations & Testimonies

*Many of these stories are brutally blunt
and tragically true. They are written
not to shock but to reveal real situations
that women have faced and celebrated
victory over with the help of their
always-faithful Heavenly Father.*

# The Stuff Inside My Old Couch

My uterus fell out in his hands. He's my husband now, and I truly believe that God gave him to me. One year before I met him, I had a baby by my first husband, a son who died in my arms. He was buried with $465. I couldn't afford a casket, so my son was literally buried inside of a little wooden box. No one on either side of my family helped me with the funeral arrangements or with any financial assistance. There weren't many people at the funeral, and the few that were there only came so that they could have something to talk about. I heard my mother whisper to my sister, "Look at him; he looks like an old man in a coffin."

When I was in the fourth grade, my best friend and I robbed her mother's bar daily. We would get drunk off the best liquor, because her mom only drank the best liquor. By the time I reached the fifth grade, I had become an alcoholic prostitute.

My mom didn't seem to like the girls in our family (her daughters); she always "played us" (my sisters and me) against each other. She seemed to relate to males better, especially handsome men. When my brother got out of jail, my mother gave him a big party. Sometimes I wonder why "our people" are so "backward." We had young people in our family who didn't get that kind of party when they graduated from college or when they came back from fighting in Vietnam.

My mother was also extremely "color struck" (meaning that she liked people who had lighter colored skin more than she liked dark skinned people). She especially liked white people, so I used to steal face bleaching cream from drug stores, and I used the bleaching cream all over my body. I even thought about using Clorox bleach on my skin to lighten it.

Everyday, my mom would call me names like, "dummy," "the slow one in the family," "slut," "hussy," "prostitute," "black as tar," "retarded nigger," and "nigger trouble."

I was in the second grade when my mother first said that I would never have babies. I wasn't having sex in the second grade yet; but I started when my mother began calling me names and giving me "the evil eye," piercing dirty looks that I still remember today.

The first person I had sex with was my father. I found out later that he was my stepfather. He raped me repeatedly, vaginally and anally; sometimes I would be so exhausted that I would collapse on our old raggedy couch and couldn't move for days. There were times when I thought that I would bleed to death.

I always believed that my mother always knew about us having sex; that's probably why she hated me so much. A couple of times—before I finally left home—my mother actually walked in on us, but she would act just like she didn't see him. The only "thing" my mother saw was the ugly, nasty pain of her own past.

I really didn't find out what some of the mean names my mother called me meant until I was 40 years old. It took just that long to become "healed enough" to think about my past.

I remember eating a lot, because I believed that if I gained weight, I wouldn't look like a whore. Also, food was very comforting, a substitute for love, in the beginning; however, food became my enemy later, because whenever I wanted to control a situation in my life or try to solve a problem, I would use food as a tool. My weight would fluctuate, back and forth, until I was unable to control my diet and until I was unhealthy from the bouncing "bouts" of my body weight.

I always vowed that if I ever had children, I would never call them derogatory names. It's the same as cursing their lives. It's the same as dictating their future, because you're actually speaking things into existence. Words are powerful; God *"spoke"* the world into existence. I vowed that I would always call my children names that were positive and uplifting. I vowed that I would love my children and encourage them every day.

In the fourth grade, my boyfriend got shot. I had nightmares about it for a long time. I used to think that he was the lucky one, because living was so hard; dying seemed easy. I was such an angry little girl, I would pick a fight with anyone who was available. I had so much anger inside of me that I didn't care what happened to anyone else or myself.

At night, I would cry myself to sleep. I don't remember a night when I didn't cry myself to sleep. I used to wonder, "Where is God?" "Who is God?" When I was being raped by my father, I always called out to God, but He never answered my call. I felt that God just didn't love me.

When my father was raping me, I would always say, "Please come help me, Jesus; please come help right now." My father would laugh heartily and say, "Jesus can't help you. No one can help you right now. Right now, I am God Almighty, and you will praise this (pointed to his penis)."

When we got home from school or came home from any place, my mother would say to us (me and my sisters), "Girls, take off those 'draws' and let me smell 'em." I always washed my panties at my girlfriend's house before I went home for the night. Sex, violence, and hatred were the things I understood best–they were "ways and means" of survival for me.

Of course, I had low self-esteem; therefore, as soon as I was old enough, I married a man who beat me regularly, every day of the week. One day, my husband threw his dirty underwear on the living room floor and said to me, "You better clean this house, spotless, but you better not touch my underwear in the middle of the floor."

## Control

I really wish that I could ask someone, "What's up with underwear? What's the 'thing' with panties and boxers?" I just didn't get it, but underwear had some special connotation that I couldn't figure out!

I felt like "Mrs. Celie" in *The Color Purple*. Her issues surrounded "the mailbox," but her problems all started with the abuse and rape by her father. My issues surrounded "dirty underwear," but my problems all started with the abuse of my mother and the rape of my father. Maybe it was all a form of control.

My neighbor used to have a dog. The dog was very mean, so they tied him up to a short leash. The length of the leash was just long enough to allow the dog to make a complete circle around his dog-house; sometimes, he would get choked around that leash, and his owner had to untangle him.

That dog used to be so angry and so determined to break that leash that he had made a complete circular groove in the ground around his doghouse, and there was no grass at all inside the circle. He would bark furiously; he was angry, because he couldn't break his leash.

After many years passed, though, that dog didn't try to break that leash anymore. He didn't bark anymore or make circles around that doghouse anymore. However, the worn-down circular area around his doghouse appeared permanent; grass wouldn't grow inside the circle.

One day, his owner (master) untied the dog and set him free, but the dog didn't know what to do. He was so used to being bound, "institutionalized," that even after he was "set free," he still never left that circled area around his doghouse.

His master tried for several weeks to get his dog to leave that invisible circle boundary. He tried to coax him out with food. He tried to tempt him out with cats; his owner even used big juicy steaks to lure the dog away from that "set circle," but the dog never left that circle—his spirit had been broken.

That dog lived and died within the "ways and means" that had been set for him for so many years. I guess "you can't teach an old dog new tricks."

At that time though, I kept thinking to myself, "Maybe God *can* help me. Even the dogs eat the crumbs which fall from the Master's table."

After several months, my husband's underwear was still in the middle of the living room floor—the same spot—even when we had company visiting. Once, we had a semi-formal dinner party, and his underwear was in the same place throughout the entire party. My husband even hired professional carpet cleaners to vacuum and shampoo the carpet, but he strictly told them not to move his dirty underwear from the middle of the living room floor.

One day, I was keeping my girlfriend's toddler, and the baby picked up my husband's dirty underwear. Obviously, the baby figured, "You're always taking off my dirty 'do do' underwear, so I better help out and pick up those dirty ones in the middle of the floor and put 'em in the dirty clothes hamper," and the baby did just that.

Of course, I took the underwear out of the hamper and tried to place them back on the living room floor the same way that my husband placed them originally. However, when my husband got home, he immediately noticed that the underwear had been moved, and he beat me to the brink of death; then, he placed those same dirty underwear in the middle of the living room floor again.

### *Hope*

After that, whenever I could, I would spend nights at my girlfriend's house or at the local battered women's shelter. Once I was watching Oprah. She appeared to be implying that some women attract abusive men; they seem to fall into the same abusive cycle, over and over again, because that's the way of life they understand. I guess it was like the dog that never left the circle. What Oprah said made a lot of sense. I believe that she was speaking about generational curses.

I had been told for years that I was basically "nothing." Sometimes, even today, I can still hear my mother screaming, "You ain't nothing, and you ain't never going to be nothing either, ugly, black nigger!"

She fed me that kind of negative stuff for years, so many years that…"I expected to be nothing," or "have nothing in life."

I felt like that stuff stuck to the bottom of my dirty, blue jean bookbag; I felt like that stuff inside our old raggedy couch. Underneath the pillows of that same dirty old couch (which my father had raped me on so many times) was lots of lint and trash, pieces of old homework that I tried to hide, leaky broken pens and pencils (that left stains which were impossible to remove), sticky candy, cigarette wrappers, cigarette butts, popcorn kernels, crumpled potato chips, broken rubber bands, broken combs with missing teeth, torn-up pictures, and a pair of my bloody underwear that I was trying to hide. Everything inside that couch was broken; nothing was "whole" or useful. Our couch was always filled with trash; there was "no money" inside that old worn-out couch.

I truly believed that my mother hated herself, and because I was a mirror image of her, she hated me too. Her hate for me was more than the hate that she had for anyone else, because I was her "younger self" with opportunities that she missed taking advantage of.

After my baby died, I found a room at a boarding house. One night, I was listening to a minister on the radio. I didn't have a television. I heard the minister say that anyone could call his talk show and receive prayer. I didn't have a telephone, so I ran downstairs to the nearest pay phone. I called the minister, and told him that I was going to kill myself, but he said that he was too busy and that he didn't have time to talk to me, because he was getting ready to leave the radio station. I was devastated! After that, I didn't trust preachers anymore. Evidently, all he wanted was money, just like so many other preachers.

That same night, I attempted to commit suicide and was rushed to the emergency room. I never found out who called 911 for me; I've tried for many years to find out, and I still don't know who called. It could have been a robber who had a change of heart after he saw that I was lying in a pool of my own blood, just waiting to die. I was told that it was a man's voice, but no one knew who the man was. Maybe it was an angel.

When I got to the hospital, I met someone whom I will never forget—a nurse who said that she prayed for me as soon as I came into the emergency room. I couldn't understand how or why she would pray for me. I was a "nobody." Why would she waste her prayers on me?

She was a soft-spoken woman who talked to me about Jesus, but I was extremely bitter at that time and didn't want to hear anything that she had to say. I told her that people who say that they are Christians…just want money and that I didn't believe "nothing" (anything) that she was saying.

Although I was very mean and nasty to her, the soft-spoken nurse kept trying to tell me about her Jesus. By my third day in the hospital, I began to be a little more polite to her, and I started listening to her story.

She told me that her father had raped her and that she tried to commit suicide too. I was so shocked, because she seemed so happy and so clean. I asked her how she succeeded in life; I was so curious about how she became so joyful and so free.

She happily told me her story. She said that years ago someone in the emergency room helped her by sharing their testimony with her. She also said that a Christian nurse once said to her, "Nothing is too hard for God. Acquire inward peace, and thousands around you will be saved!" The nurse's testimony gave me some "new found" peace and even a little joy.

I didn't want to leave the hospital, because I was still afraid to face the world again, alone. When it was time for me to be discharged, the nurse said a special prayer for me; she told me that she believed God had a special "work" for me to do. She also said that…one day, I will tell others my story. I'll always remember her saying, "Nothing is too hard for God!"

After I was discharged, I called my ex-husband, but he wasn't at home; his best friend answered the telephone and offered to come and pick me up.

When he came to the hospital, he told me that he had some shocking news to tell me. He told me that my ex-husband had been involved in a horrible accident and that he was in a coma. I had mixed emotions, but my ex-husband's best friend was there to hold my hand through it all.

My husband's friend was an extremely quiet person; I was very glad that he came to pick me up from the hospital. I didn't know him very well at that time, and I was afraid of anyone who seemed "too good to be true."

He made sure that I was safe inside my boarding room and went out to get me some food and other things that I needed. He was so nice, it was scary. I'd never met anyone like him before. He checked on me daily, and one day, he told me that he had special feelings for me.

I, of course, didn't trust him or any other man, so I quite naturally tried to run him away by laughing in his face and cursing him out regularly. I was so mean to him that if he didn't truly care, he would have definitely left me alone.

I would never call him or be home when he told me that he would come to visit me. I would curse him out, and I even tried to start a fight with him, because fighting is the way I learned to settle things. Violence and hatred were the two things that I understood best.

Finally, I met a lady on the street who told me that God had sent me a husband. She said, "There is a man, already in your life, and he loves you very much; you are going to marry him, and you will receive many children, not of your own."

Surprisingly, she didn't ask me for money, but it was still too good to be true. However, as I began to look back over my life, I said to myself, "Obviously, God loves me. He sent some mysterious man to call 911 when I tried to commit suicide. God also sent a nurse to tell me her testimony, and now this lady, whom I never met before, is saying that God has sent me a husband."

### *Love*

I called up my admirer for the first time, and I asked him, "Were you the one who called 911?" He answered, "No, but I believe that God sent an angel your way." He told me that he loved me and asked if he could come over, because he had something to ask me.

I allowed him to come over which was a rarity, and he said that he loved me and wanted to marry me. I wasn't ready to give him an answer, but within the following weeks, he showed me more love than I ever had in my whole life. He never touched me, and he always respected me in every way; he respected my body and my soul. He convinced me that he loved me, and he convinced me to marry him.

We both became Christians, and we got married. About nine months later, my uterus literally fell out into his hands. I went to the doctor and was told that I would never be able to physically have children.

However, about three years later, God began sending us children.

My husband and I have seven children now. God had a master plan. It may have appeared that I was cursed "not to have children," but God was in control of the situation. God knew what He wanted us to do. His plan will always still be fulfilled. All our children were adopted, but they are still "all our children." The word "adopted" only means "chosen." We believe that God chose us to be their parents, and God chose them to be our children. There is "nothing" too hard for God!

God allowed us to adopt children who had special needs. Some were abused (raped by family members); as a result, they were filled with anger like I was. However, the beauty of all this pain is the fact that I am able to relate to them and care for them in the special way that they need care, love, and healing.

We have four beautiful, virtuous girls and three handsome, God-fearing boys. I never call my children cruel names. Sometimes, our whole family gets together to see how many *good* names we can call each other. It's so comforting to finally be a member of a functional family. I am so happy!

My husband and I watch over our children like hawks, and I believe that we are raising them in a manner that pleases God. They all have surrendered their lives to Christ, and one day, I hope that they will "tell their story" (testimony) to help others and continue glorifying God.

I thank God that He sent someone to my boarding room that day; I believe that He sent a special angel to save my life.

Today, I volunteer at battered women's shelters. I spread the word of God to everyone I see, and I sincerely hope that my testimony helps someone else to heal, the way that wonderful nurse helped me. I will praise and worship Jesus Christ for the rest of my life. I have forgiven all the people who hurt me in the past, and I pray for them daily.

I'll also tell my story to anyone who will listen, because God spared my life so that I could help others tell their story. The things that we "go through" are not for us; we endure and suffer to help others.

No matter what happens in your life (even during the most painful situation), please remember that "God is in control!" Regardless of how bad things look in the beginning, God will take care of you, because there is nothing too hard for God.

Today, my sister, allow your Father God to heal you. You are His daughter, and He loves you with all His heart! I'm so glad that I have a Father who loves me.

Although incest is tragically the best kept secret in America, God still knows about every incestuous occurrence. God knows how many strands of hair are on our heads. He knows our deepest thoughts that we often hide from people closest to us. God even knows how your life-story will end, and He wants you to continue to walk in your divine destiny! Today is the day! Walk in your divine purpose with Him!

Sincerely,
*A Woman of Divine Destiny*

## *Grandma Joy's P.S.*

It may be very painful and extremely difficult to express your personal feelings and past hurts, but perhaps a little easier to write. Have you ever begged for attention from your mother, but she denied you the time and love you so desperately needed? Have you ever tried to confront your mother with an issue, but instead of listening and comforting you, she told you that you were a liar? Did her denial and rejection cause you to become bitter? Are you angry? Do you hold resentment? Do you need healing? Please pray first; then, write down your feelings about the story you just read.

_____

_____

_____

_____

Would you forgive a relative (such as your father) for molesting you? What would you say to a father who has committed such sins? What would you say to a seemingly unloving mother who has failed to protect you?

_____

_____

_____

_____

_____

## Scripture Analogies

Your Heavenly Father has given you Scriptures that will heal and strengthen you. In fact, God has given you a special word of comfort and peace. Please pray first; then, read these Scriptures and write down your thoughts concerning His Word and your personal situation.

### JEREMIAH 17:14

*Heal me, O Lord, and I shall be healed; save me, and I shall be saved: for thou art my praise.*

_____

_____

_____

_____

### ROMANS 8:28

*And we know that all things work together for good to them that love God, to them who are the called according to his purpose.*

_____

_____

_____

_____

### LUKE 19:10

*For the Son of man is come to seek and to save that which was lost.*

_____

_____

_____

_____

_____

### EPHESIANS 2:8-9

*For by grace are ye saved through faith; and that not of yourselves: it is the gift of God: Not of works, lest any man should boast.*

---

---

---

---

### 2 CORINTHIANS 5:17

*Therefore if any man be in Christ, he is a new creature: old things are passed away; behold, all things are become new.*

---

---

---

---

### PSALM 147:3

*He healeth the broken in heart, and bindeth up their wounds.*

---

---

---

---

### EPHESIANS 2:4-5

*But God, who is rich in mercy, for His great love wherewith He loved us, Even when we were dead in sins, hath quickened us together with Christ, (by grace ye are saved).*

---

---

---

## PSALM 37:1-15

*Fret not thyself because of evildoers, neither be thou envious against the workers of iniquity.*

*For they shall soon be cut down like the grass, and wither as the green herb. Trust in the Lord, and do good; so shalt thou dwell in the land, and verily thou shalt be fed. Delight thyself also in the Lord; and he shall give thee the desires of thine heart.* (In your Bible, please continue reading Psalm 37 to verse 15.)

_____

_____

_____

_____

## 2 CORINTHIANS 10:3-5

*For though we walk in the flesh, we do not war after the flesh: (For the weapons of our warfare are not carnal, but mighty through God to the pulling down of strong holds;) Casting down imaginations, and every high thing that exalteth itself against the knowledge of God, and bringing into captivity every thought to the obedience of Christ.*

_____

_____

_____

_____

## JOHN 3:16

*For God so loved the world, that He gave His only begotten Son, that whosoever believeth in Him should not perish, but have everlasting life.*

_____

_____

_____

_____

Now, think of a time when God has delivered *you* from something painful (anything you can think of), or think of something good that God has done in your life.

_____

_____

_____

_____

_____

_____

Write the things that you must do in order to continue to walk in faith and please God.

_____

_____

_____

_____

_____

_____

Please remember that your past pain will be a testimony for someone else who is presently suffering from a similar situation. You will glorify God when you share your testimony.

*Laughter is good medicine!*
(See Proverbs 17:22.)

*Throughout this book, you'll find
funny stories that will make you smile.
Here's the first one:*

ৡৱ

# Dear Lord

A little boy wanted $100 badly and prayed for weeks but nothing happened. Then, he decided to write a letter to the Lord requesting the $100. When the postal authorities received the letter addressed to the Lord, USA, they decided to send it to the President.

The President was so impressed, touched, and amused that he instructed his secretary to send the little boy a $5 bill. The President thought this would appear to be a lot of money to a little boy.

The little boy was delighted with the $5. He sat down and wrote a thank you note to the Lord, which read:

Dear Lord,
Thank you very much for sending me the money. However, I noticed that for some reason you had to send it through Washington, DC, and as usual, those thieving politicians deducted $95.

### *Reflection:*

We must learn to forgive others regardless of the pain we feel they have caused us. Our sins cannot be forgiven unless we forgive others.

LUKE 3:12-13

*Then, tax collectors also came to be baptized, and said to Him, "Teacher, what shall we do?" And He said to them, "Collect no more than what is appointed for you." (NKJV)*

_____

_____

_____

_____

PHILIPPIANS 4:19

*But my God shall supply all your need according to his riches in glory by Christ Jesus.*

_____

_____

_____

_____

*The following is another extremely touching true story about a woman who became addicted to alcohol and other drugs. There may be many who will always condemn her for her sins, but God has forgiven her. After reading this story, imagine that God has directed you to go and visit her in prison. What would you say to her? Would you encourage her or give up on her? How would you treat an alcoholic family member who became a robber and a prostitute? Have you experienced anything similar to her story?*

ॐ

# I Am an Alcoholic

I stood before the crowd for the first time to tell my story. I had listened to others, and it was time for me to share my story with them.

My name is Star, and I am...an alcoholic. Before coming to the Alcoholics Anonymous program, my life was completely out of control, and I don't believe that I could have reached the internal peace and the external success that I was seeking before I gave my life to Christ and came to this Alcoholics Anonymous program.

Before I recognized the fact that I was an alcoholic, I had a job which paid a great salary and a wonderful family, a husband and children who loved me dearly. My life seemed perfect; at first, I was drinking to fit in socially, to keep up with the crowd, and to help me not be so shy and inhibited.

We always had big parties at work, and drinking quickly became the common bond that we all shared together when we were stressed out from work. We believed that the more a person worked, the more they deserved to drink. Of course, I cannot blame anyone but myself. I've learned from Alcoholics Anonymous that I cannot shift the blame, but that I must take responsibility for my own actions and for my own drinking and drug problems.

Every day, after working nine or ten hours, I'd sit at my favorite hangout spot (a local bar) and try to drink my problems away. In the beginning, I was a "functioning alcoholic," meaning I could get up and go to work and do the things that I needed to do as a wife and mother too.

However, after a while, I couldn't go home without being drunk. When I was younger, I always used to say, "Why do people drink and drive? It's crazy!" As crazy as it was, it's exactly what I was doing. I wasn't facing my problems. I considered myself to be a social drinker who had the ability to quit at any time, but the truth was far from that. I was an alcoholic, and to ask someone to drive me home would be too close to admitting that I had a drinking problem.

So I took a chance every night, driving myself home from bars. A couple of times, I almost had a car accident, but that wasn't what gave me "the wake-up call." That wasn't what made me confess, "I am an alcoholic!" Losing my job, as well as losing my family (husband and children), going to prison, and having no one to call on but God…forced me to admit that I am an alcoholic. I had to hit "rock bottom" first!

But, before I admitted that I am alcoholic, I was hanging out on the corner like a lost puppy. When I couldn't seem to drink enough to hide from my pain, I started taking drugs. I tried cocaine and crack cocaine.

That's when I began to stop going home. I had no desire to be a wife and mother. Most of the time, I didn't even have a clue where I was. Everything seemed to happen overnight. My life began to spiral out of control in an instant, and I felt hopeless.

One morning, I woke up in a ditch stark naked. I didn't have a stitch of clothes on; I didn't know where my purse was or even where I was. I was lost, and didn't even remember my own address or telephone number. All I remembered was that I wanted to get high. I craved getting high more than I wanted to live, more than I even wanted to breathe. I would have sold my soul for a hit.

If it weren't for a police officer, I wouldn't have made it home. He said that my family had reported me missing months ago. I didn't even remember the night before; how could I remember months before that day?

The police officer was obviously someone I knew. He must have recognized me; he kept saying, "Oh my God, I can't believe it. Oh my God, I can't believe it." I asked him where or how did he know me. He told me that he knew me from church. He said, "You used to teach Sunday school." After he mentioned it, I remembered going to church, but I was so embarrassed that I replied, "I definitely never taught Sunday school."

He took me home; my husband was at work. My oldest daughter was at home babysitting my 2-year-old daughter. My oldest daughter cried profusely when she first saw me; then, she collected herself and went to run me some bath water and make me something to eat. I could hear her praying while she was cooking. While she was busy cooking me some food, I picked up my 2-year-old daughter and headed out the door, still naked as a "jay bird."

I didn't have any money, but I had planned to sell my youngest daughter for some money or some drugs, whichever came first. I saw a man on the street; I wasn't sure if I had seen him before, but he seemed to know me. He gave me $5 and his coat; he said that he didn't want to buy my baby.

I told him that it wasn't enough money, but it was either all he had or all he could give me. I, at least, had enough to catch the bus back to my old stomping grounds where the drugs were. I used to think that drug addicts were poor, ignorant people who lived in neighborhoods away from us decent, civilized folks who had jobs and families who loved us.

Well, the truth is far from that. People of all walks of life such as doctors, pastors, teachers, police officers, and pharmacists are addicted to drugs, and that addiction is such a powerful force that it can change anyone; *addiction can drive a pastor to steal, kill, and destroy.*

When I got back to my old stomping grounds, I asked everyone I saw if they wanted to buy my baby. No one wanted to buy her, so I decided to prostitute my body out the same way I had done so many times before. Since I wasn't able to sell my baby immediately, I decided to prostitute her body out too; then, afterward, I planned to get as much money as I could get from anyone willing to buy her.

A man gave me $10 to perform oral sex with him and his dog, but he said that he didn't want to have sex with my baby while I watched. I asked the man (a perfect stranger) if he wanted to take my baby home to have sex with her. He took her, and that's the last time I saw her.

I was so desperate for a hit that I didn't care where he took my child or what he did to her. He only gave me $10; I guess that was the total payment for having sex with him and his dog *as well as payment for my daughter's life.*

Before I could get my next hit (smoke more crack), someone came from around a dark corner of the street and held a gun to my head and stole all my money from me. It wasn't much money anyway; except, now, after the robbery, I was broke and very desperate. I would do anything to get my next hit. I didn't care what I had to do. I didn't care if I went to prison or not, so I broke into a couple of stores.

I was caught by the police trying to break into the cash register of a store owned by people who used to be very good friends of our family. My ex-best friends thought that my action was an effort to hurt them personally. They came to see me while I was in prison and expressed the fact that they hoped that I burn in hell forever.

At the time, I hadn't been spiritually delivered, and I didn't even understand my actions, myself; therefore I couldn't explain the fact that I am an addict, an alcoholic, and I didn't know how to tell them about the characteristics of a desperate addict. An addict who is not receiving treatment is prone to do anything, including murdering someone; *an addict who is not receiving treatment will do anything!*

***Always remember that the stem of a crack pipe is very narrow, but everything you own will pass through it.*** When you take your first hit, you've made a deal (signed a contract) with the devil.

It took going to prison and losing everything, absolutely everything in my life (hitting rock bottom)for me to get to the place where I am today...to the place where I can say that "I am an alcoholic, and I need help."

(Weeping intensely) Telling my story is not as hard as having to hear it myself. The world judges me harshly, but I judge myself even harsher! I go over it all in my head, daily, and I ask myself, "How?" and "What would make me sell the body and life of my own child?"

While I was a little girl, my grandmother used to say to me, "A star can only be seen in darkness. When it is midnight, stars shine bright. Trust God when there is no light anywhere except in heaven. God will lead and guide you. He will cause you to shine, even in the middle of the darkest night!"

Only God can help me now! My family and friends have all given up on me, but God hasn't!

I will learn to trust God, and He will help me. He will lead and guide me through the storms and the dark night, and through my testimony, I will shine. I will be that star that people see in the darkest of the night. I am God's star here on earth, and through me, God will shine!

In my personal experience with the Twelve-Step Program, I have found there are two important keys for improving my spiritual life and spiritual growth. One thing is prayer and the other is honesty.

My prayer is: "God, I offer myself to you, **to build me and do with me as you will.** Please relieve me of the bondage of self that I may better do your will. Take away my difficulties, that victory over them may bear witness to those I would help with your power, your love, and with my new way of life. **May I do your will always!**"

This is a prayer of surrender of yourself and all your rights and belongings to God to do with as He pleases. Because God is smarter than us, and loves us more than we love ourselves, He will always do a better job running our lives than we can do for ourselves. If you are an alcoholic, surrender yourself to God. He *will* come to your rescue.

Sincerely,
*A Woman of Divine Destiny*

## Grandma Joy's P.S.

Alcohol is the most widely used and abused drug in America! When people begin the difficult struggle to overcome addiction, they often feel alone in their struggle and as if everyone has given up on them. If you feel that way, know that you are not alone and that not everyone has given up. Please don't feel alone or powerless—there are people like you who care about your well-being.

Most of those who have succeeded in the Alcoholics Anonymous program attribute their success to the spiritual nature of the Twelve-Step Program. These are the ones who thank God for their release from addiction slavery. They know their release was beyond their ability, because they often sought self-healing by their own willpower that always failed them. Freedom from addiction came only after they joined Alcoholics Anonymous and followed the Twelve-Step Program.

The testimonies of those who have "made the program" always give credit for their success to their "Higher Power," God, as seen in Step Five.

Alcoholics Anonymous® is a fellowship of men and women who share their experience, strength, and hope with each other that they may solve their common problem and help others to recover from alcoholism. The only requirement for membership is a desire to stop drinking.

*How would you treat a church member*
*who was once lost but has received*
*amazing grace (salvation) from God?*
*What can wash away (all) our sins?*
*Nothing but the blood of Jesus!*

✌

# The Blood of Jesus

One night in a church service, a young woman felt the tug of God at her heart. She responded to God's call and accepted Jesus as her Lord and Savior. The young woman had a very horrible past, involving alcohol, drugs, and prostitution. But the change in her was evident.

As time went on, she became a faithful member of the church. She eventually became involved in the ministry, teaching young children. It was not very long until this faithful young woman had caught the eye and heart of the pastor's son. The relationship grew, and they began to make wedding plans.

During this time the gossipers began stirring up trouble and causing problems for them. You see, about half of the church did not think that a woman with a past such as hers was a suitable wife for a pastor's son. The church began to argue and fight about the matter so they decided to have a meeting.

As the people made their arguments and tensions increased, the meeting was getting completely out of hand. The young woman became very upset about all the things being brought up about her past. The church members were even using her personal testimonies against her.

As she began to cry, the pastor's son stood to speak. He could not bear the pain it was causing his wife-to-be. This is his statement:

"My fiancé's past is not what is on trial here. What you are questioning is the ability of the blood of Jesus to wash away sins. Today, you have put the blood of Jesus on trial. So, I am here to ask you, does Jesus' blood wash away sins or not?"

The whole church began to weep as they realized that they had been slandering the blood of the Lord Jesus Christ.

Too often, even as Christians, we bring up the past and use it as a weapon against our brothers and sisters. We Christians too often want to play judge and jury. Forgiveness is a very foundational part of the Gospel of our Lord Jesus Christ. If the blood of Jesus does not cleanse the other person completely, then it cannot cleanse us completely either. If that is the case, then we are all in a lot of trouble.

What can wash away my sins? Nothing but the blood of Jesus! End of case!

God is a "second chance" God! *"Cast your burden upon the Lord, and He shall sustain you. He shall never suffer the righteous to be moved"* (Ps. 55:22 NKJV).

Romans 6:6 tells you that the old woman—the woman who was molested, abused, demeaned, or rejected—died with Christ! That woman who was filled with fornication, adultery, abortion, drugs, alcohol, lusts, bitterness, and unforgiveness died with Christ, and we know this because: *"While we were sinners, Jesus Christ died for us"* (Rom. 5:8).

It's time to walk in your divine destiny! This is your season, and the harvest is plentiful!

*The following story involves a conversation with
two men, a doctor, and his male patient.
Women are able to read this true story and "listen"
to two men having a private conversation about sex,
sexually transmitted diseases, and unfaithfulness.*

දැ

# I Can't Get AIDS

A man went to see a doctor about a private problem he was having. "I don't know what I've gotten a hold of, doctor," laughed the man. The doctor asked the man (his patient), "Are you married?"

"Yes, that's why I drove this great distance to be seen by you. I've been married for over 25 years. Surely my wife and I have a family doctor, but I didn't want to take any chances that might lead to getting caught or risk my wife possibly finding out anything."

The doctor asked, "So, you're saying that you do have sexual relations with someone other than your wife?"

"Yes, I do. Doesn't every married man at one time or another?" said the man, mockingly.

"With how many?" asked the doctor.

"Well, that's kind of hard to say; I'm not quite sure, but I do get my share of fun and excitement!" said the man.

"How about your wife, does she have sexual relations with someone other than you?" asked the doctor.

"Why, of course not! My wife would never do anything like that. I know my wife very well, and I know that she wouldn't dream of having an affair; she wouldn't dare have sex with anyone else," stated the man.

"The truth is that she has slept with every person you have slept with. You've exposed her to as much danger as you've exposed yourself to," stated the doctor.

"Well, you don't quite understand; I don't mess around with dirty women. I would never touch a dirty woman. I only deal with clean women," said the man, in a very concerned tone.

"Do you have unprotected sex with them?" asked the doctor.

"Sometimes, yes, but I take good care of myself; that's why I'm here," said the man.

"You're here because you think that you might have a sexually transmitted disease. *AIDS is also a sexually transmitted disease*, and there are lots of other STDs. You can't look at a women and tell if she has an STD," said the doctor.

The doctor was able to convince the man to take an HIV test. The test results were positive—the man had HIV.

Everyone is different, as every situation is different. This is a true story, and like so many others, it does not have a fairytale ending. However, this story may help to save someone's life! AIDS doesn't discriminate; *anyone* can get AIDS—the young, the old, the married, the single, the rich, the poor, as well as every race, creed, and culture.

(Every major city has a clinic that is equipped to confidentially give you an HIV test as well as provide you with information about HIV and other sexually transmitted diseases.)

## *Personal Feelings*

Have you ever been betrayed by a boyfriend or husband? What feelings come to your mind when you see these words?

anger

---

trust

---

disappointment

_____

hope

_____

love

_____

### Scripture Analogies

The following Scriptures will heal and strengthen you. In fact, God has given you a special word to comfort and heal you. Please pray first; then, read these Scriptures and write down your thoughts concerning them and your personal situation...

PSALM 103:3

_____

_____

ACTS 10:38

_____

_____

ISAIAH 53:5

_____

_____

PSALM 147:3

_____

_____

ISAIAH 57:18

_____

_____

Now, think of a time when God delivered you from something painful (anything), or think of something good that God has done in your life.

_____

_____

_____

_____

Write the things that you must do in order to continue to walk in faith and please God.

_____

_____

_____

_____

Please remember that your past pain will be a testimony for some-one else who is presently suffering from a similar situation. You will glorify God when you share your testimony.

*Laughter is good medicine!*

❧

# A Wife's Promise

There was a man who had worked all of his life, had saved all of his money, and was a real miser when it came to his money. Just before he died, he said to his wife, "When I die, I want you to take all my money and put it in the casket with me. I want to take my money to the afterlife with me."

And so he got his wife to promise him with all of her heart that when he died, she would put all of the money in the casket with him.

Well, he died. He was stretched out in the casket, his wife was sitting there in black, and her friend was sitting next to her. When they finished the ceremony, just before the undertakers got ready to close the casket, the wife said, "Wait just a minute!"

She had a box with her. She went over with the box and put it in the casket.

Then the undertakers locked the casket down, and they rolled it away. Her friend said, "Girl, I know you weren't fool enough to put all that money in there with your husband."

The loyal wife replied, "Listen, I can't go back on my word. I promised him that I was going to put that money in that casket with him."

"You mean to tell me that you put all that money in the casket with him!?" asked her friend.

"I sure did," said the wife, "I got it all together, put it into my account and wrote him a check. If he can cash it, he can spend it."

*The following story is fictitious,*
*but it provides an excellent analogy*
*of our Lord's will for us and our desire to*
*hold on to material things that have no value!*

ℱ

# The Bag Lady

On an extremely cold winter night, a bag lady stood between two shopping carts, shivering in the cold, holding her shopping carts tightly, one in each hand. An attendant from a nearby shelter asked her to come in for some hot soup and stay at the shelter for the night. She immediately said, "Oh, yes, help me with my things." Pleasantly with a big smile on her face, she began to try to push one cart and looked back at the attendant, expecting him to push the other one. "I can't push both of them; they are just a little bit too heavy for me," she said excitedly.

To the bag lady's dismay, the attendant said, "I'm sorry, we only have enough room for you, not your two shopping carts. You can take some important things with you that will fit in your pocket like pictures, identification cards, telephone numbers, or medicine."

The bag lady was disappointed, but tried not to show it. She replied, "That's ridiculous; these are all my earthy possessions. They are all important to me. If I leave my two carts out here overnight, someone will surely steal everything I own."

"I'm sorry, but those are the rules, ma'am. It's going to be a very cold night. If you change your mind, here's my card (gives her his card). I'm just three doors down from this corner. If you knock at the door, I'll let you in," said the attendant. After realizing that the attendant was not going to change his mind, she replied, "I've survived many cold nights, much worse weather. Tonight will be just like any other night. I can take care of myself. I'll be just fine."

The attendant went back to the shelter and thought about the bag lady most of the night. He kept hoping that she was going to show up, but she didn't. "Maybe she found another shelter, or maybe someone saw her and took her home," he thought. Early the next morning, he rushed down to the corner to check on her. Running from a distance, he could see the two shopping carts, but could not see the bag lady. "Obviously, she finally left her two shopping carts to seek warm shelter," he thought.

Nevertheless, when the attendant got close enough, he could see the bag lady's body lying between the two shopping carts. She had frozen to death in an effort to safeguard all her earthly possessions. The attendant was grief-stricken and confused. "I wonder what was so important it was worth dying for?" he thought.

He carefully checked the shopping carts, each had newspapers neatly folded over the top. In an effort to hide her possessions, the bag lady covered her two shopping carts with newspapers instead of using the newspapers to keep herself warm during the extremely cold night.

Underneath the newspapers, the attendant found only rusted tin cans and broken glass. He was sure that there must have been something that he was overlooking, so he carefully and respectfully searched her body. All he found was the card that he had given her. The address and telephone number of the shelter was written on the back the business card. On the front were the words, *"For what is a man profited, if he shall gain the whole world, and lose his own soul?"* (Matt. 16:26)?

### Reflection

One way of looking at the story is to see all the good things that God offers, things we don't always notice because we're so busy holding on to trash. Although initially the bag lady quickly agreed to the idea of staying in the shelter overnight, she changed her mind when she found out that she couldn't bring all her baggage and trash with her.

In the beginning, people are often willing to submit their lives to Christ; nevertheless, when they have to be obedient and make sacrifices, they change their minds, thinking that they will be losing something worthwhile. They feel that the sacrifice is too great and decide to stay out in the cold with their worldly possessions. Wouldn't it be fantastic if they knew that they were only steps away from saving their lives?

If you think for a moment of Jesus as being the attendant, you can see that He (like the attendant) couldn't make the bag lady come into the shelter for safety; He could only supply the good news. The bag lady had to make her own decision. Like the attendant, Jesus cared about her and promised not to turn her away if she knocked at the door. He only required that she give up a few things, some things which are necessary to leave behind when you come into the shelter; God is the shelter in the storm. When you enter God's shelter, there are some things that you can't take with you. People can replace all the junk, but they can't replace their lives.

The bag lady appeared to be debating whether to leave her belongings and go into the shelter for safety, or whether she should risk staying out in the cold. However, her final decision was based on her own ability; she said, "I've survived many cold nights, much worse weather. Tonight will be just like any other night. I can take care of myself. I'll be just fine."

We must come to the realization that we can't make it on our own. The bag lady was depending on her own strength instead of depending on God. Everyday, we are faced with life-changing decisions such as whether to "cleave to the world" and all we think that the world has to offer or come in from the unbearable cold and allow the Lord to take care of us. Surely, there are some people who will ask, "Why would anyone lose their life to protect *worthless material things, especially trash?*"

Well, you're probably familiar with the old saying, "One man's trash is another man's treasure." She truly believed that her possessions were extremely valuable. Even if she had been truly monetarily rich, "For what is a man profited, if he shall gain the whole world, and lose his soul?"

## *Scripture readings*

- ✧ Matthew 16:26
- ✧ Matthew 6:19-21
- ✧ Matthew 6:33

# Eagles in a Storm

Did you know that an eagle senses when a storm is approaching long before it breaks?

The eagle will fly to some high spot and wait for the winds to come. When the storm hits, it sets its wings so that the wind will pick it up and lift it above the storm. While the storm rages below, the eagle is soaring above it.

The eagle does not escape the storm. It simply uses the storm to lift it higher. It rises on the winds that bring the storm.

When the storms of life come upon us—and all of us will experience them—we can rise above them by setting our minds and our belief toward God. The storms do not have to overcome us. We can allow God's power to lift us above them.

God enables us to ride the winds of the storm that bring sickness, tragedy, failure, and disappointment in our lives. We can soar above the storm.

Remember, it is not the burdens of life that weigh us down, it is how we handle the burdens that will take us through to victory over them.

# Extreme Wedding Shower

Jacob, age 92, and Rebecca, age 89, living in Florida, were all excited about their decision to get married. They went for a stroll to discuss the wedding and on the way they passed a drugstore. Jacob suggested they go in.

Jacob addressed the man behind the counter: "Are you the owner?"

The pharmacist answered, "Yes."

Jacob: "We're about to get married. Do you sell heart medication?"

Pharmacist: "Of course we do."

Jacob: "How about medicine for circulation?"

Pharmacist: "All kinds."

Jacob: "Medicine for rheumatism and scoliosis?"

Pharmacist: "Definitely."

Jacob: "How about Viagra?"

Pharmacist: "Of course."

Jacob: "Medicine for memory problems, arthritis, jaundice, indigestion, and gas?"

Pharmacist: "Yes, a large variety. We have the works."

Jacob: "What about vitamins, sleeping pills, Geritol, antidotes for Parkinson's disease?"

Pharmacist: "Absolutely."

Jacob: "You sell wheelchairs and walkers?"

Pharmacist: "All speeds and sizes."

Jacob: "Great! We'd like to use this store as our Bridal Registry!"

*For some people, abortion is a very touchy subject;*
*for others, it appears to be "no big deal."*
*This story gives you an opportunity to see two*
*different perspectives about this controversial*
*subject. A young woman and an elderly*
*woman both confront the issue of abortion.*

ℱᴈ

# I Cannot Kill My Baby!

I was throwing up a lot; however, I was in denial. I had taken about five pregnancy tests that showed positive results before I finally decided to go to the doctor. I told him that I had already made up my mind…that I definitely wanted to have an abortion. He calmly said that I have choices and gave me some information.

The word "choices" is such a peaceful word, but what does it really mean? The dictionary says that it means, "the power, right or liberty of choosing; having options, a sufficient number or variety from which to choose."

At first, having choices seemed great! I get to choose! But it was the hardest thing I'd ever tried to do.

For a while, I thought about adoption, but I was afraid that my child would grow up, find me, and hate me for the rest of his/her life for putting him/her up for adoption.

I decided that I would abort my baby. That's right; I chose to get rid of this situation. I wasn't married. I was a dedicated member of my church, but I didn't even have a boyfriend. I got pregnant by a "one night stand." I'm not usually promiscuous, that's why I didn't have any birth control. I wasn't sexually active with anyone else and didn't expect to be anytime soon.

My partner said that he had taken a precaution—I'm not sure if that was true now. I guess that's all water under the bridge anyway. I was almost 30 years old and pregnant by someone whom I really didn't even know.

I was so mixed up, so confused, that I felt it would have all been better if I had been raped. Then, I would be able to have an abortion without the hassle of feeling guilty. Anyway, babies don't feel when they are aborted...I don't think. I'll have an abortion before the baby can feel anything.

I called an abortion clinic and scheduled an appointment. They told me that I couldn't be more than four months pregnant. I was sure that I wasn't four months pregnant yet.

When the day of my appointment came, everyone was "snowed in." Everything, all appointments, had to be cancelled and rescheduled for a later date.

I was angry, but I was still determined, so I rescheduled my appointment. It was hard for me to find someone who would drive me there and stay with me throughout the ordeal; it was hard to find someone who would not "judge me" or tell the whole world my business. I asked my kind, elderly neighbor to take me to the abortion clinic—she thought she was just taking me to have a "check-up."

When I arrived for my appointment, I saw people picketing, lots of people with signs and flyers. One lady picketer said to me, "God doesn't want you to have this abortion. He already knows your baby's name and what your baby will look like. You're supposed to have a healthy baby girl, if you don't kill her first."

The other picketers were shouting at me, saying, "Murderer! Murderer!"

My neighbor figured out what was going on and told me that she didn't want any part of the abortion. During the ride back home, my neighbor began to cry, profusely. I asked her what was wrong, and she told me that years ago she had an abortion. It was illegal back then, and she was left unable to have children afterward. She said that when it's quiet at night, she could hear her baby crying.

She pulled the car over, and I went into a store to buy her some water. Inside the store, I saw this beautiful little girl. She looked up at me and said, "You're going to have a little baby?" I replied, "Yes, I'm going to have a little baby."

I went back to the car and told my elderly neighbor and friend that she was in "no shape to drive," so I took the wheel and drove us home. My neighbor continued to talk about her abortion and how horrible it made her feel, even today. She said that she felt that God was punishing her for having an abortion; she said, "That's the reason why He never allowed me to have any children. I would do anything to reverse what I did. If only I had made the right choice! How could I ever have chosen to kill my baby?"

I said to her, "God has forgiven you, and He has your name written in the Lamb's Book of Life!" I felt that I had to say something to console her; she was obviously filled with lots of guilt and pain.

"God doesn't want you to have an abortion," she pleaded. "Please, listen to me, He doesn't want you to have the abortion!"

After seeing her so torn and hearing her story, I couldn't bear to get rid of my baby at that time. Who could? At that time, I felt that there was no way I could have an abortion. I decided to wait a while and think things over.

Yet, as I got farther along and could barely hide the fact that I was pregnant, I decided that I had to do something fast, before everyone on earth found out that I was pregnant. I was more determined than ever to have an abortion. I decided that I would drive myself to my next scheduled appointment, if possible.

I was so torn, but I tried to rationalize with myself by thinking things like, "I'm not the only person in the world who will ever have an abortion. Everyone doesn't feel like my neighbor. Plenty of other women have had abortions, and they went on with their lives."

I rescheduled another appointment. But on the day of my appointment, when I was walking down the stairs from my apartment, I fell and twisted both of my ankles. Of course, my nosey neighbor called the ambulance, and they took me to the hospital.

At the hospital, I was given a sonogram test to see if my baby was all right or see if the fall had hurt the baby. I didn't want to look at the sonogram, but the doctor kept saying, "Look, look at your baby," so I did. "Do you want to know the gender," the doctor asked? I said, "Yes, I guess it won't matter." The doctor told me that I was having a little baby girl. I looked and saw my little baby girl.

Tears rolled down my face, as I thought to myself, "I cannot kill my baby! I don't have that choice to make. It's God's decision, not my choice to make!"

"Do you have any names for her," a nurse asked me. I said, "I want to name her Mary. My neighbor's name is Mary. She will be pleased that I named the baby after her."

I couldn't stop crying or looking at the picture of my baby. She was moving around. She was real. I almost killed her, but she is still alive and well, because of the divine purpose of God. She's my Mary, and God knows her name. God knows my baby girl's name, and I'm glad that I did not kill my baby!

Sincerely,
*A Women of Divine Destiny*

### *Grandma Joy's P.S.*

Some people say that having an abortion is a choice—a decision that they can make to get rid of their baby. But, what would Jesus say? What choice did His mother Mary make? Are you willing to allow God to steer and guide you in the right direction? God has a divine purpose for you and your baby. Today is the day! Walk in your divine destiny with Him!

*The following story will inspire and encourage you, regardless of what you're going through. You'll know that "there is nothing too hard for God," and—in turn—there is nothing too difficult for a woman who is determined to "take it all back!"*

ൟ

# Taking It Back

Don't get in my way because I'm throwing punches, and I'm aiming to knock the devil right out! I told the devil to give me back my family and our blessings in no uncertain terms! I said, "I demand that you take your hands off my family!"

I got tired! That's exactly what happened. I was fed up, and I wasn't going to take it anymore! It was time for me to reclaim everything that the enemy stole from me!

But before that time, I was not a prayer warrior, and my husband was having an affair with someone he met on the internet. Our teenage daughter ran away with a man ten years older than she was, and our son was heavily on drugs and in trouble with the law.

When all these things began to happen, and my life began to crumble before my very eyes, I became depressed, so depressed that I thought about committing suicide.

But then I remembered my grandmother's prayers. She was a prayer warrior! She always said, "Baby, it's a war in here (pointing to her heart), but God already has the victory. All we need to do is stay on the winning side! This war is different, because this war is inside your mind and in your heart. It's a war inside all of us; that's where the real war is!"

At that time, I didn't have a clue about what my grandmother was saying. She died before I got married. I got married as soon as I graduated high school.

I was raised in church. We used to have a fire-burning, holy time in church, and I thought that I knew God, because we always had a good ole' time in church. I became a Christian when I was only 15 years old, and I never had much to worry about. My Christian walk was a breeze. My faith was never tested; therefore, I had no reason to become strong or no reason to learn how to depend on God.

I have been married for more than 16 years. We have two beautiful children and supportive family and friends.

My husband had a prestigious, prosperous career, and we had a beautiful home. I was a timid housewife and mother. I never worked outside of our home. My job was to "keep appearances." My husband wasn't going to church, but I managed to somehow maintain some form of contact with the church for political purposes (namesake purposes and to keep up appearances).

If anyone asked us what church we belonged to, we had an answer, and that was important…to belong someplace. I hadn't been studying the word of God outside of church. Even though our family appeared normal…like "we were one big, fat, happy family," I was gripped with fear inside my heart and inside my spirit.

That's how it all got started. It started with a little seed of fear that was somehow planted in my spirit, and my life began to spin out of control. (What I didn't understand at the time, was that we—my family and myself—weren't covered with the blood of Jesus. We had no protection. *Anything* could have happened to us!)

Every day, for a whole year, something extremely terrible happened. Our family suffered so much. We lost our house, because my husband lost his job. My daughter became pregnant, but she lost the baby. My son was in prison, and he lost his opportunity to attend his top-choice college. And, I lost my joy. I had no strength or willpower. I had the biggest pity party anyone could ever throw for herself.

Now, for the first time in my life, I had to "get down and dirty" with that low-down thief, the devil. As I looked at our family portraits, I realized that I had to be strong. I began to realize that I wasn't dead yet! Instead, I was just "fed up," and I wasn't going to take it anymore! I decided that my family and I had seen and experienced enough pain and that I had to be the intercessor. I had to become the mediator, the source of strength for the whole family. It was my job to take back everything that the enemy tried to steal from us!

The problem was: How was I going to be that source of strength? The enemy was trying to take over, what could I do about it? I wasn't equipped to fight the enemy. I had no prior fighting experience. Now, without my grandmother and no experience, how would I fight the enemy?

I decided to *try* God for myself! I began to read God's Word, and like a child, I believed everything God said. I decided to stand on the promises of my Christ, my Savior, like the words of the old hymn we used to sing in church. I read God's word and prayed without ceasing, and I began to apply it to our family life. Besides, I figured that Jesus gave us His word for a reason. It was time that I fought that battle my grandmother used to tell me about.

While everyone was whispering about me and laughing at me, I began turning my plate down (fasting), and I began to speak peace into our lives.

One day, while I was on my knees praying, my furniture was being repossessed. Even my prayer altar was taken from under my kneeling body.

A couple of weeks later, while I was in my yard praising God, a man with a tow truck came to repossess my car. It took me another month to find a "piece of car" to drive, but I found a clunker, and I drove that old clunker hoopty-car until it finally stopped running. It was loud and spit out a lot of smoke, but for a long time, it got me where I needed to go.

My neighbors were whispering about me like Job's friends gossiped about him. They said, "You must have done something extremely wrong for God to punish you so severely."

The critical judgment of others and their laughter would have made my situation an extremely humiliating experience, but it wasn't embarrassing at all (by this stage of my life), because "by now" I had found the peace that surpassed everyone's understanding. No one understood why I was still so "on fire" for Jesus.

I continued to praise God, except now, I was praising God everywhere, even in the middle of parking lots. One day I was praising God in the middle of Wal-Mart's parking lot and my praise and worship attracted several people to come and praise God with me.

I began to pray like never before! I began shouting and praising God in the middle of grocery stores. I didn't wait until the battle was over; I went ahead and began shouting the victory! I didn't care what the situation looked like. I told the devil to get out of my way, because I was coming through with a two-edged sword, and I was taking back my family and our peace that he tried to steal and hold hostage.

One morning, while I was "praying without ceasing," another truck pulled up to our house. I told the driver that he must be mistaken, because there was nothing left in my house to repossess. The driver calmly said, "Lady, your husband called me to come and move his belongings. He said he was moving or something like that."

Even though it seemed that things couldn't possibly get any worse, my husband announced that he was leaving to go and live with his teenage lover. Later that afternoon, I saw my husband with her. They were arm and arm, kissing each other. The enemy thought that he had me, but seeing them together only made me fight harder. It made me mad with the devil, and I was more determined than ever to stand strong and firm; I became a fighter!

Just when I thought that the enemy couldn't take anything else, he tried to steal my heart; he tried to break my spirit. But my spirit wasn't broken. Before this time, the enemy was stealing only tangible, material things. Now, the enemy was sending out the spirits of oppression, depression, poverty, adultery, and division.

A month later is when my son was incarcerated, another month later is when my daughter ran away and called to say that she was pregnant.

Now my marriage was gone, and my children were gone and in trouble.

I won't lie to you, I cried at first! I cried and cried, but something inside of me wouldn't let go. I refused to quit! Jesus was trying to "birth" a new spirit inside of me. He wanted to make me a prayer warrior! The process wasn't easy, but it was inevitable. It had to be done. I had been stagnant too long, and it was time for me to grow strong in the Lord. Before all these events happened, I was like a tree that was not bearing fruit. God wanted me to bear fruit, so he began to cultivate and purge me. He began to cut away all the dead limbs, and he began to shake me so that I might bear fruit. The process wasn't easy, it was painful, but I became closer to God like never before!

Jesus wiped my tears and told me not to worry, because He was proud of me and had a divine purpose for me. I began to pray and praise God like never before. I fasted, prayed, and worshiped God that whole week, and I went to church that Sunday. I was so "on fire" for God that I began praising God before I found my seat. My praise ignited the dead spirit in the believers and sparked the spirits of non-believers as well. My praise was contagious!

I began to fight again. It was a battle, but God already had the victory. All I had to do was stay on the winning side! All I had to do was keep claiming the victory because the true war was inside my mind. *The true battle wasn't physical, it was a battle between believing and not believing.*

Another month later was when I received the foreclosure notice for my home. For some reason, though, I wasn't afraid anymore, like I was when I was just "playing church" and just "going through the motions" that hypocrites go through.

Again, the enemy thought that he had me. However, by this time, I was cunning; I was sharp; I was wise as a serpent and gentle as a dove. I told him that God was still in control and that we have already won. It's a fixed fight! We are the winners!

Even though I had never had a job before in my whole life, I applied for a job at Wal-Mart and was hired. It wasn't long before I became a store manager and eventually a district manager.

Jesus gave me the wisdom and power to take back my life by storm! Everywhere I went, I shouted, "Glory to God, I'm taking it back!"

The enemy tried to creep into my mind, but by now, he was a joke to me. He knew that I was a fighter! Any time, he tried to show his ugly head, I'd shout at the top of my lungs, "In the name of Jesus, I'm taking it back! I'm taking it back! I'm taking it back!"

I was not the scared, timid little wife and mother anymore! I was a prayer warrior! I lifted up my house to God; my house became a house of praise! I didn't care who heard me. I wanted people to hear me, because I was constantly shouting and praising God!

By the time I got in touch with my daughter, she had accepted Jesus as her Savior and wanted to come home!

A month later, my son was out on probation and had become a Christian!

A month later, my husband came home and had become a Christian!

I stood steadfast! I was a true believer, and God sent my husband and children back home to me. He and our children are Christians now! Every obstacle that the enemy placed in front of me was removed.

I'm here to say to you…that if the enemy is robbing you of the life that God wants you to have, it's time to take back your life! Take back your family! Go now, woman of divine destiny, and take it all back!

Sincerely,
*A Woman of Divine Destiny*

## Grandma Joy's P.S.

Anger is natural reaction to painful situations, but harboring anger and resentment stops the hand of God. The key is to not allow the seeds of anger to ever become implanted. The trick is to immediately begin telling God what happened; immediately let God know that you believe that it is His responsibility to show you how to respond to the painful situation. God wants you to depend and lean on *Him.*

Don't ever give yourself room to react and get angry. Don't ever allow room to build up a house of bitterness. Instead, begin to humbly confess your anger to God and ask Him to direct your path. Explain to the Lord that you came to Him quickly because you didn't want to have to handle the situation alone, and because you knew that you couldn't do it alone. When you place all your feelings, every emotion, in God's hands, you become strong enough to "take back" everything that you thought you lost to the enemy.

Fill in the blanks...

I have learned

_____

_____

I believe that

_____

_____

I am not afraid

_____

_____

**Read Psalm 37:1-15 and fill yourself with God's promises.**

Also remember 2 Corinthians 10:3-5:

*For though we walk in the flesh, we do not war after the flesh: (For the weapons of our warfare are not carnal, but mighty through God to the pulling down of strong holds;) Casting down imaginations, and every high thing that exalteth itself against the knowledge of God, and bringing into captivity every thought to the obedience of Christ.*

*Laughter is good medicine!*

ॐ

# Greener Grass

Two cows were grazing in a field. The curious cow said to the other, "The grass sure looks greener, on the other side; I want to know why. Is it really better? I must know! I must get to the other side!"

The other cow said, "How would you get over there? The fence is made of barbed-wire." The curious cow said, "I'm the smartest cow around. I'll find a way to get over the fence. No one can stop me!"

Each day, the curious cow tried to figure out a way to get across the fence. He thought of nothing but the green grass on the other side. He was so worried and preoccupied with this thought that he wouldn't eat or sleep. He became weak and got very sick.

One day the farmers came to get the curious cow; they took him to the other side and buried him. The curious cow finally made it to the other side. Now we know why the grass always looks greener on the other side!

### Reflection

Although we're just talking about cows in this story, the message is clear! Analogously, there are people who worry themselves "sick" because of material things that they want and can't have. Of course, the grass often looks greener on the other side! But, "peace of mind" is better than all the riches in the world!

*The following story reveals a sin that is
"all too common," the sin of adultery.
When adultery is committed, everyone loses
something—and some things are lost forever.*

✿

# In Love With a Married Man

I used to always say, "I'll never date a married man," but I did. I dated a married man and fell in love with him or "thought" that I was in love with him.

We met at work, and we started out as "just friends." However, our job required us to be alone together and discuss matters for hours, and we gradually became lovers. We used to laugh and eat together on our lunch breaks. Sometimes, if I didn't bring lunch, he would give me his lunch, the lunch that his wife cooked for him; sometimes, it was their "leftovers," dinner his wife and children ate the night before.

I knew he was married from the very beginning. It was never a secret. He never tried to hide it, and he wouldn't have been able to hide it anyway, because we work with very nosey people and live in a small town. Also, he talked about his wife and children a lot.

I think he liked me because I was exciting; he could talk to me about all the things that he couldn't talk to his wife about. He could also do with me...all the things that he couldn't do with his wife. He used to compliment me on how nice I looked when I came to work.

Once he said to me, "I wish that my wife would dress like you." Of course, I didn't have sense enough to know that it was just a "come on" line. He used other "come on" lines like, "My wife and I haven't been getting along for a long time. I'm seriously thinking about leaving; the only reason I'm still around is because of the children. I am going to get a divorce, because my wife is not a good wife and mother. I'm sick of doing everything by myself. My wife and I don't have sex. I don't know the last time my wife and I had sex. We don't even sleep in the same bed together. Things definitely aren't going well at home for me. One day my wife is going to look for me and I'll be gone! I need someone, a good woman, who will appreciate me. I'm tired of being in a relationship with someone who doesn't excite me or appreciate me."

I absolutely hate it when I ask a married man if he's married and he says, "If you want to call it that." Once, I had a man reply to the question by saying, "I'm there; she's there too, but it ain't exactly what you would call a marriage. But if that's what you call it, fine." Another favorite answer is, "I'm still married, but we're not together; we're separated!" Another extremely popular answer is, "I caught my wife cheating on me!" Or, men will say, "She moved out, and moved in with her mother. I don't know why she left. I was working two jobs, trying to take care of her and the kids, and she still wasn't satisfied. I caught her cheating with my best friend. I believe that she was even messing 'round with my brother. She had a good 'thang' going, cause I'm a good man." Men act like answering that question is so hard—a man is either married or he's not married!

Why do men who commit adultery always say that their wives are "the worst wives in the world?" Yet the men I knew who were committing adultery always claimed that they were such good husbands to wives who didn't deserve them. Before having this affair, other married men (who were already having affairs) used to approach me with the same old sob stories. They would always claim that their wives were terrible—that she wouldn't cook, clean, and didn't take care of the kids. I guess they tell those lies to gain the sympathy of the woman they are pursuing, if she's dumb enough to believe everything that the adulterer and/or whoremonger is saying. Some men can tell some very persuasive lies; their lies can be extremely convincing.

Well, I was dumb enough to believe those lies for a while, and I became an adulterer myself. Now, looking back, I can say that I was extremely blind, and I am godly sorry for my actions.

I never called his home telephone. I definitely knew not to do that. I always called him on his cell phone. If he answered his cell phone, and she was in the room with him, he'd let me know by saying, "I'll talk to you later; call me back later." One thing is for sure; if I ever get married, I'm going to check my husband's cell phone frequently. I tell every married woman I meet to check her husband's cell phone.

My married lover and I would have sex all the time. We did it as many times as we could. He and I would often "play hooky" from work by calling in "sick," or we would just take a day off work and be together while his wife thought he was at work. Every week, we sat down together with our schedules to try to find a day when we both could get off work.

In the beginning, he tried not to disrupt his normal schedule too much. He made sure that he didn't do anything that seemed abnormal or suspicious. In other words, we couldn't date normally; we couldn't go out to a restaurant and see a movie. We had to sneak around, and hiding wasn't always easy. After a while, though, we became a bit relaxed, and we didn't hide like we did when we first met.

Once we even made love in their bed while his wife was visiting her parents. That's when I began feeling guilty and couldn't sleep at night anymore. I couldn't eat, and I felt weighed down. I was seriously depressed, but for some reason, it didn't seem to phase him a bit. Maybe it was because he had already had previous affairs, maybe numerous affairs.

He told me that his wife's best friend mentioned something about him having an affair, because she had seen him with me on several occasions. But he said that he swore to his wife that he wasn't having an affair. He said that his wife believed him and that she has stopped talking to her best friend, whom she believes is trying to ruin her marriage.

The whole affair became depressing, and I thought that I'd feel better if we had more sex. I tried to do all the things that his wife wouldn't do. I tried to be all the things that his wife wouldn't be. I have to admit that I felt extremely guilty. Sometimes, I would go to church and the preacher would be preaching about adultery. It seemed like the preacher was talking directly to me. It seemed as though he knew that I was committing adultery, because he would look at me "dead in the eye." So, for a while, I just stopped going to church.

I had never been "without a man" before, and I felt better "sharing a man" than not having a man at all. Ever since I was old enough to date, I'd been involved with or had some type of a relationship with a man. I was one of those women who felt that she "had to have a man" or she didn't feel complete.

However, I was being tormented daily; the affair was a burden. I tried to bury my guilt as best I could. It was easy to do when we were having sex, but it was hard to do when we weren't together. I felt an empty feeling; it was a horrible feeling. I had fallen in love with a married man, a man that couldn't possibly ever be mine. I'm willing to give anyone (who will listen) some advice: It is dangerous to sleep with married men, because it hurts everyone involved. It unleashes dangerous emotions and feelings that you shouldn't be feeling.

We had a Christmas party at work. I don't know what possessed me to go, but I went. My lover was there with his wife and children. His wife, unaware that I was in love with her husband, sat down beside me and talked to me; her husband (my lover) was not nervous at all; she was bragging about how much of a "good husband" he was. Part of me felt sorry for her, but another part of me was angry; that part of me wanted to tell her all about her so-called "good husband." I wanted to tell her that her "good" husband was really my man!

I didn't say much, just "Hello," but I was "checking her out" from head to toe. I expected her to be a big, fat, out-of-shape, unhealthy woman. I expected her to be wearing a dress that looked like it was made from old curtains or that she would be wearing a big sloppy t-shirt with writing on the front. I thought maybe her feet would be swollen, possibly looking like she was baking bread inside of her shoes.

I envisioned her wearing no make-up or jewelry and her hair looking a mess. I figured that she never visited the beauty parlor and that her hands and fingernails would look like she chopped wood for a living.

Contrary to all I envisioned, his wife was beautiful. She was absolutely stunning. Moreover, her eyes shined bright; it was clear that he was the apple of her eye. It was even clearer that because she was such a beautiful woman that he (my lover and her husband) was a selfish whore who lied about everything.

I thought that his wife would be a big fat joke; instead of laughing at her, I was upset, hurt, and jealous. While sitting there watching this pretty picture-perfect family, I tried to put some things into perspective. First, I thought, "If he was unfaithful to her (a beautiful wife of many years and the mother of his children), he would surely be unfaithful to me if I could ever possibly take him from her."

Next, I thought to myself, "Look at him; he would never leave his family. So what was I doing in the picture? The only thing that we could ever have together is a physical relationship. I may have fallen in love and would do anything for him, but he didn't have those same feelings about me. It's clear by looking at them…that what we have together is nothing at all!"

I felt foolish and wished that I had never met him. While I couldn't change the past, I surely had the power to change the future.

That next Sunday, I went to church and confessed my sins to the pastor. He and his wife counseled me, and his wife gave me some videotapes. The tapes were recordings from the ministries of Dr. Juanita Bynum and Dr. Joyce Meyer.

After watching the videotapes and after receiving counsel and guidance from my pastor and his wife, I decided that I had to let my married lover go! I fell on my knees and asked Christ to save my soul. I was forgiven for all my sinful, adulterous acts. However, I was still deeply hurting, and it took some time for me to heal emotionally. But God is a healer and a deliverer. I sought God with all my heart, and He comforted my spirit.

Unfortunately, though, my ex-lover and his wife got a divorce, because she found out about our affair. His wife and children moved to another state. My ex-lover lost his job. Our lives were changed forever! When adultery is committed, everyone loses something! *Sin carries an expensive price with it.*

Everywhere I go, I tell women the truth. The truth is that sin can be temporarily exciting, but it's all just a trick of the enemy. My situation clearly proves this. A similar example would be a situation in which a woman (who confesses Christianity while she's in church) is asking God for a husband, yet she is still having sex with her live-in lover.

She is caught up in a whirl-wind of lust. She is "mimicking" the role of a virtuous Christian woman by going to church and praising God for giving her this ungodly relationship which she has been involved in for several years, even before she became a Christian. However, her own guilt and sin separates her from having a true and intimate relationship that she desires to have with the Lord. She's actually having a spiritual heart attack. She wants a break-through, but she isn't willing to stop fornicating with her lover. Sex before marriage is a trap. Adultery is a trap.

Marriage is honorable in the sight of God, but adultery is an abomination. The very relationship that we have with our Father God and His son, Jesus, *is based on a spiritual marriage, not a physical one.* Jesus said that when we accept Him as our personal Savior, we become united (married) by the covenant promises of God.

Once Jesus is united with you, you have a bond forever with Him, and He will never leave you or forsake you. A Christian might backslide and leave Him, but He will always remain a faithful Bridegroom until the end, because Jesus is married to the backslider. If you're confused about relationships and marriage, read the Bible. Before you go out and spend a huge amount of money on legal fees, before someone in the relationship is heartbroken, and before rela-tionships are ruined, read the Word of God.

The Bible is a true "law book." It has the way, the truth, and the life in the Scriptures (John 14:6), and no one should get married without reading and following the biblical law. For all the single women read-ers, just remember that you are not alone, because Jesus is with you, and He gives you perfect love, a love that *no man can give you.*

Sincerely,
*A Woman of Divine Destiny*

## Grandma Joy's P.S.

All marriages don't end happily after adultery has been committed. Also, sometimes women and men both harbor anger and resentment after adultery has been committed or after a divorce. Instead of being able to resolve a relationship or dissolve one with closure (with some peace of mind), a wife or husband might allow seeds of bitterness to grow and fester in their spirit. Bitterness often hinders people from having (future) healthy relationships, intimate or platonic.

It may be very painful and extremely difficult to discuss but perhaps a little easier to write. Pray first, and then write down your feelings about this story…Be honest! If you are angry, it is okay to express your anger. Remember that harboring anger and resentment blocks your blessings. You'll unblock your blessings by expressing your feelings and by humbly asking God to take control of your emotions.

What have I lost?

_____

_____

What have I gained?

_____

_____

What will happen to me?

_____

_____

## Scripture Analogies

Reading Scriptures will heal and strengthen you. In fact, God has given you a special word to comfort and heal you. Please pray first then read these Scriptures and write down your thoughts concerning them and your personal situation.

JOHN 4:13-14

*Whosoever drinketh of this water shall thirst again: But whosoever drinketh of the water that I shall give him shall never thirst; but the water that I shall give him shall be in him a well of water springing up into everlasting life.* (Meaning that man can offer you physical water which temporarily quenches your thirst, but God offers you spiritual water that quenches your thirst forever.)

_____

_____

_____

_____

### PSALM 51:10

*Create in me a clean heart, O God, and renew a right spirit within me.* (Meaning a spirit filled with clean thoughts and right desires.)

_____

_____

_____

### JEREMIAH 6:14

*They have healed also the hurt of the daughter of my people slightly, saying, Peace, peace; when there is no peace.* (Meaning that you can't heal a wound by saying it's not there! You must first admit that there is a problem.)

_____

_____

_____

### PHILIPPIANS 3:13

*...forgetting those things which are behind, and reaching forth unto those things which are before.* (Meaning forgetting the past and looking forward to what lies ahead, the future.)

_____

_____

_____

The following Scriptures are especially for wives and their husbands.

PSALM 147:3

*He healeth the broken in heart, and bindeth up their wounds.*

---

PROVERBS 18:22

*Whoso findeth a wife findeth a good thing, and obtaineth favour of the Lord.*

---

HEBREWS 13:4

*Marriage is honourable in all, and the bed undefiled: but whoremongers and adulterers God will judge.*

---

EPHESIANS 5:22-33

*Share this Scripture with your husband. Husbands, love your wives, even as Christ also loved the church, and gave himself for it: That he might sanctify and cleanse it with the washing of water by the word, that he might present it to himself a glorious church, not having spot, or wrinkle, or any such thing; but that it should be holy and without blemish. So ought men to love their wives as their own bodies. He that loveth his wife loveth himself...*(Eph. 5:25-28).

_____

_____

_____

_____

Also read and meditate on the following Scriptures:

- ❧ John 8:7
- ❧ John 8:11
- ❧ Romans 12:2
- ❧ Isaiah 9:4

Now, think of a time when God has delivered you from something painful (anything), or think of something good that God has done in your life.

_____

_____

_____

_____

Write the things that you must do in order to continue to walk in faith and please God.

_____

_____

_____

_____

Please remember that your past pain will be a testimony for someone else who is presently suffering from a similar situation. You will glorify God when you share your testimony.

# Little Johnny Tells All

Little Johnny watched his daddy's car pass by the school playground and go into the woods. Curious, he followed the car and saw Daddy and Aunt Janie in a passionate embrace. Little Johnny found this so exciting that he could not contain himself as he ran home and started to tell his mother, "Mommy, I was at the playground, and I saw Daddy's car go into the woods with Aunt Janie. I went back to look, and he was giving Aunt Janie a big kiss, then he helped her with her shirt buttons. Then Aunt Janie helped Daddy unbuckle his belt. Then, Aunt Janie…"

At this point, Mommy cut him off, and said, "Johnny, this is such an interesting story, suppose you save the rest of it for suppertime tonight. I want to see the look on Daddy's face when you tell it tonight!"

At last, it was dinnertime. At the dinner table, Mommy asked Johnny to tell his story. Little Johnny started his story, "I was at the playground, and I saw Daddy's car go into the woods with Aunt Janie. I went back to look, and he was giving Aunt Janie a big kiss; then, he helped her with her shirt buttons. Then Aunt Janie helped Daddy unbuckle his belt; then, Aunt Janie and Daddy started doing the same thing that Mommy and Uncle Bill used to do when Daddy was away in the Army."

## *Moral*

Sometimes you need to listen to the whole story before you interrupt!

*"You can't fool your mother."*

ℰ∂

# Platonic Relationship

A young man assured his mother (over the telephone) that he and his girlfriend were living together but not sleeping together.

His mother decided to visit him and his girlfriend. When his mother arrived, she saw that the couple had two separate beds, and her son assured her again that he and his girlfriend had a platonic relationship.

The mother left but wasn't convinced that they weren't sleeping together. His girlfriend noticed that their good silverware was missing after his mother left. She said, "I'm not trying to accuse your mother of stealing, but it's mighty strange that our good silverware walked out when she left. You need to call her and ask her about our silverware."

The young man was hesitant to do so, but he finally called his mother and asked her if she knew anything about their good silverware.

The mother kindly replied, "If things were as you said, *she would know that I put the good silverware in her bed, under the sheets.*"

*A good mother is hard to find.*
*We all make mistakes, but*
*a good mother is one who allows*
*God to lead and guide her!*

ℱə

# Shortening Bread

There once lived a devoted, Christian woman. Every morning, she would pray, sing, and bake shortening bread. When she finished baking her bread, she would leave it on the window ledge to cool. The aroma of fresh baked shortening bread would fill the air, and an old homeless man would come by and eat her shortening bread. Every morning, for years, as soon as she would bake the bread and sit it out to cool, the homeless man would come by and eat it.

"I am tired of that old homeless man stealing my shortening bread, and I am going to do something about it. He should get out and find a job," grumbled the woman to herself. As she said the words, she became very angry. The more she spoke, the more upset she became. She became so angry that she decided to teach him a lesson. "I know what I'm going to do. I'm going to poison him! I will fill the next mixture of shortening bread with poison," said the woman.

As she put the ingredients together, all kinds of thoughts ran through her mind. She thought about all the times that she, herself, had done wrong and had been forgiven. She thought about her prayers that morning—she had asked the Lord to give her an opportunity to bless someone. She even thought about a long lost loved one that she missed and prayed would safely return.

Tears began to run down her cheeks as she realized that she could not kill another human being. "I cannot kill that man. What was I thinking? I have to love my neighbor as myself," said the Christian woman. She had a change of heart and decided to throw away the poison bread mixture and bake some fresh shortening bread just for the old homeless man. "I'll use my best ingredients and bake him the best shortening bread that he's ever tasted," said the woman.

This time, instead of being angry, she sang gospel songs. She stirred, baked, and prayed until she had baked the most delicious shortening bread that anyone could ever bake. "Dear God, in the name of Jesus, forgive me of all my sins, and please bless this shortening bread. May it be used for your glory. Thank you for giving me an opportunity to bless this homeless man," prayed the woman, as she placed the bread on the ledge of the window. She waited, and once more the homeless man smelled the aroma, came by, and picked up the shortening bread.

"Oh my goodness! She usually only gives me one shortening bread a day. She has already given me one today. I'm very full, but I don't want to hurt her feelings. She surely must be a good Christian woman to give someone like me two breads in one day. It is hard to believe that someone cares about me. No one else has ever loved me enough to do anything like this. I often hear her singing and praising her God. Well, surely, there must be a God, a lovely God! I believe that the God whom she serves loves me! Maybe He wants me to serve Him too! That's what I'll do! I'll serve Him too! Although I am full, I do not want to hurt her feelings, and I do not want to disappoint my new master. He must be a wonderful God to be able to love a person who doesn't have a job, home, or a family. I'll just take this blessed bread and share it with others," said the homeless man.

The homeless man felt God's love and was very happy. He decided that he would go into the city and share the blessed bread and God's love with everyone. On his way into the city, he saw a young fellow who appeared to be starving to death. The young man could barely speak. "Don't try to talk, you have to regain your strength. I have some blessed bread that a good Christian woman gave me. It is a sign that God loves us. Here, eat all you want," said the homeless man. The young fellow ate the bread and regained his strength. "Thank you, kind sir, for that blessed bread," said the young fellow, and he continued his journey into the village.

The homeless man continued his journey into the city. When he arrived, he told everyone of the good news. "I know of a good God. He truly loves us all. A good Christian woman showed me His love by giving me some blessed bread. Come one, come all; you are all welcome to eat of this blessed bread," shouted the homeless man, as he prayed and broke bread for everyone. One by one, everyone in the city came. Young men, old men, old women, young women, children, preachers, teachers, doctors, expectant mothers, sick people, poor people, rich people, and homeless people came. All who were sick received healing. All who were hungry were fed. All who were homeless received jobs and purchased themselves homes. But, most of all, everyone who was lost received salvation! Everyone rejoiced, and all who had breath praised God!

The man, who was once homeless, now had a job, a house, and a wife. He was very thankful. He continued to praise and serve God.

In the meantime, in the village, the good Christian woman stared out of the window. "I sure am glad that I had a change of heart. Something tells me that the shortening bread has surely been a blessing for someone. Thank you, Jesus. I know that you have answered all my prayers," said the Christian woman.

Just before the Christian woman began to close her window, she saw a miracle. "It' a miracle! It's a miracle! Glory to God!" shouted the Christian woman, as she ran to the door. She opened the door and embraced a young man who was standing on the other side. "Mother, Mother, I'm so glad that I made it back home, but I would have starved to death if it weren't for an old homeless man who gave me some blessed shortening bread that some good Christian woman and her God gave him. I'm so glad God loves me!" said her son. (*He was her only son, and he had been away from home for many years.*)

*Here's a story about a woman who tells us why she had to sit on the back row of the church and how it made her feel.*

# Sitting In the Back Row of the Church

Years ago, when I got pregnant, I had to sit in the back row of our church. Back then, the rule was…if you got pregnant, and you were unmarried, you were confined to the back row of the church, and you couldn't socialize with the so-called "untainted" Christians in the congregation.

When the church service ended, you didn't have to go straight home, but you had to get the heck out of the church because you weren't allowed to stay after church to hug and talk to the other members. You were excommunicated until you had your baby and until the congregation decided that you'd learned your lesson about fornication or adultery.

The women wore their best outfits and their biggest hats to match in hope to "look holy and sanctified." They believed that if they appeared "sickly saved" in the face that they would look more holy (like they had been fasting all week).

In our church, the women weren't allowed to wear lipstick or any kind of makeup. We couldn't press our hair or perm it (straighten it). We couldn't wear pants; also our dresses had to be a certain length, and we couldn't wear the color red, because it was "too loud" and was considered a "jezebel color."

If anyone walked in with any kind of makeup on, they were immediately confronted (in the most harsh manner possible) by mothers of the church. The mothers called all makeup "rouge." They pronounced it "rouuuuge." "Take off that rouuuuge! It's the devil's clay!" they'd say in a manner that surely humiliated whoever they were addressing.

The Bible says that we should come to church as we are. I wonder if anyone has read that part of the Bible? What if someone walks in "off the street?" Well, that has happened, and the person was immediately washed and redressed, and they still had to sit on the back row because they were considered tainted, unworthy to have contact with the so-called righteous veteran saints.

Why wouldn't a woman want to look her best and be happy in church? Why would anyone want to look sickly saved?

They (the "right kind" of Christians, mainly women) were paraded in by the ushers, and they sat in the front rows of the church. They had their heads in the clouds, and wouldn't dare talk to an outcast like me. They were too embarrassed to even look at me. I guess they felt that if they looked at me or talked to me, they would become contaminated jezebels, but the truth is that they were ignorant; most of them were just playing roles.

As soon as they walked out the door of the church, they began gossiping about who had committed sins, especially the sin of looking tacky. Wearing the wrong outfit was considered a sin, and it appeared to carry the same weight as the crime of murder. Of course, the other sin that was discussed was the sin of desire. If anyone was secretly flirting with a man or was accused of having any kind of sex with a man who was not her husband (whether it is fornication or adultery), she was taken into an interrogation room to be questioned.

Although having sex and dressing tacky were the biggest crimes, there was another that ranked almost as highly as the others—the crime of listening to or dancing to the wrong kind of music. They thought that you couldn't possibly be a Christian if you were listening to lively music.

Maybe you're wondering how I got into this fix. Well, I was born into the church, but my punishment all started with a man who sexually set me on fire. Before my relationship with him began, I was a so-called good, church-going woman. I attended every church service; I was considered a faithful church member.

The man who tempted me was so fine—he looked like hot buttered pancakes on Sunday morning. When we first had sex, I told him that I had to repent and that we could not do it again. But instead of being a good Christian, I became a hypocrite like so many others. I was still going to church, but...at the same time...I was thanking God for an ungodly relationship. Basically, I was having a spiritual heart attack.

I was asking God for a husband, while I was still going home and having sex with Johnny. I had lost the close relationship that I had with Jesus, but the physical experience that I was having with Johnny was driving me crazy. I was so mixed up, and I knew it was wrong, but I couldn't stop. I didn't know how to stop.

I kept trying to rationalize; I said to myself, "When he marries me, he'll be my husband, so it's alright to have sex with my *future* husband. I'm sure that God knows my heart."

There I was—sitting in the back row of the church, because I was pregnant and unmarried. Ironically, the man who got me pregnant was allowed to sit in the front row. Men who got women pregnant were not punished, tabooed, or confined to the back row of the church.

While I was sitting in the back row, the preacher would preach about fornication and adultery, and he would point at me. My sin was fornication, not adultery, but it didn't matter to my accusers; all they knew was that I was pregnant and not married! The preacher would say, "We can't have loose women in God's house!" The women in the front row would agree with a shout, "Amen! Hallelujah!"

In all my years of going to church, I'd never seen a sinful man confined to the back row of the church or punished in any kind of way. The rule was that the back row was reserved for sinner women only, mainly pregnant women. Also, we had to say, "woman with child," or "She made a mistake." How can they call my baby a mistake? Didn't God breathe life into my baby? Didn't God give him a soul?

You would think that someone would figure out that we women *can't get ourselves pregnant.* I guess it shows how narrow-minded some people were in those days, especially in the church. I felt torn and mixed up, but the members of the church, especially the women, weren't free to be honest with each other, and we didn't discuss our true feelings (our womanly feelings) with each other. We all pretended that we didn't have "womanly desires." Maybe if we (women) felt comfortable enough to admit to each other that we were human beings with great feelings and desires, we could have prevented some troubled times from happening.

If we could have been honest and confessed that we weren't perfect people…that we have a sinful nature and that God is our only answer, we could have rejoiced together about how He comes into our lives, saves us, ministers to us, and helps us grow in grace.

Since I was forbidden to talk to the more experienced women like the mothers of the church, I didn't have anyone to counsel me about my problems. Finally, however, my lover left, and he started attending another church where he got another woman pregnant. She (like me) was confined to the back row of the church and the cycle of ignorance started all over again with a new woman becoming an outcast.

After I had the baby, the church officials made me confess all my sins, and I was finally allowed to sit in the front row of the church. By that time, though, I had lost a lot of respect and faith for the officials who were ruling the church. I really didn't mind confessing and explaining my sins to the church. My problem was that I just didn't feel like I should be punished by men, mere human beings. I felt that *only God had the authority to judge and punish me for committing fornication.*

My fellow church members made me feel like the woman who was about to be stoned for committing adultery. Jesus said to the men who were about to stone her, "He who is without sin cast the first stone!" But, since no one was sinless, they walked away knowing that they had no right to judge or kill her for the act of adultery. (See John 8.)

I did something that I should have done long before this time; I finally confessed my sins to Jesus, and oh, what a relief I felt in my spirit. Jesus forgave me of all my sins and told me to go and sin no more!

Although it's all behind me now, I had to share my experience with you so that you don't get caught up and called out by a man who offers you nothing but physical pleasure. Also, maybe someone who is still a member of a "close-minded church" might read this and see how unproductive and painful it is to judge or punish a woman who has committed fornication or adultery. It would be better to provide counseling, love, and prayer—because we all are sinners, only saved by His grace and mercy.

Sin temporarily makes you lose your mind, but your relationship with God is more important. I will never hurt the Lord Jesus again the way I hurt Him in those days! Even if men judge and punish you for your sins, just remember that you're human and that we "all have sinned and come short" (Rom. 3:23). And even when your accusers say that you're a great sinner, because you got pregnant, and they tell you that you must sit in the back row of the church, God will listen to you when no one else will. God won't judge you the way man does, and *He'll even hear your prayers while you're saying them sitting in the back row of the church alone and pregnant.*

*The next two short stories*
*are divine messages from God to*
*daughters (of all ages) and their*
*mothers. You can also share these*
*stories with your whole family!*

ॐ

# Mother's Day

A man stopped at a flower shop to order some flowers to be wired to his mother who lived 200 miles away. As he got out of his car he noticed a young girl sitting on the curb sobbing. He asked her what was wrong and she replied, "I wanted to buy a red rose for my mother but I only have 75 cents, and a rose costs two dollars."

The man smiled and said, "Come on in with me. I'll buy you a rose." He bought the little girl her rose and ordered his own mother's flowers. As they were leaving he offered the girl a ride home.

She said, "Yes, please! You can take me to my mother."

She directed him to a cemetery, where she placed the rose on a freshly dug grave. The man returned to the flower shop, canceled the wire order, picked up a bouquet and drove 200 miles to his mother's house.

# Footprints in the Snow

A woman who was tired, blistered, and weary from working so hard prayed to the Lord: "Lord, after staying up half the night washing and ironing, I got up early and cooked breakfast for the children; then, I dressed them and sent them off to school. After that, I cleaned the house and went to work for 10 hours. Finally, after work, I walked for miles in the snow. Lord, I don't know how I ever made it."

The Lord answered her, saying, "Years ago, I was searching for someone virtuous, humble, and dedicated to bless them with beautiful children. I wanted this person to raise these children, teaching them the same qualities of virtue, humility, and dedication that you have. You made me proud! You passed every test! You've done well with the task assigned to you. Today, I knew that you would need more help to complete your assigned task. Therefore, I gave you extra strength, energy, and love."

Jesus continued to speak to her saying, "Many years ago, I laid down my life for you so that you could wake up this morning. I became poor so that you could have all your needs met. I became weak so that you could be strong enough to care for your children. I carried a heavy burden so that I could carry you all the way home in the snow. That's how you made it home. Remember, no matter how deep the snow is or how hard the wind blows, I am always with you!

"I love you and will be with you always. Please, don't ever give up. As you continue to walk in your divine destiny, I'll walk with you. And if you ever look back and see only one set of footprints in the snow, you'll know that it was when I was carrying you."

*Ladies, let's go hunting and find
out why Christians suffer...*

૪૭

# Why?

There were once two neighbors. One was a Christian, and the other wasn't. One day, the unsaved man said to the Christian man, "Why are you always suffering trials and tribulations? I'm not going through anything."

The next day, the Christian man invited his unsaved neighbor to go fishing with him. As they caught fish, the Christian man said, "Look, you caught a fish. You can't hook a dead one." The unsaved man agreed.

The next day, the Christian man invited his unsaved neighbor to go deer hunting with him. As the unsaved man tried to shoot a deer, the Christian man said, "You're targeting the best of the best. The sick ones can't run like this; they are somewhere hidden out of sight." The unsaved man agreed.

The next day, the Christian man invited his unsaved neighbor to go bird hunting with him. As the birds flew across the sky, the Christian man said, "Look at those beautiful birds fly; the weak ones are still hidden someplace in their nest. The weak ones can't soar like eagles." The unsaved man agreed.

The Christian man continued by saying, "We all want the best, and so does God. He seeks those who are running the good race, those who are not afraid to fly, and those who are not dead in the waters. Nevertheless, the enemy always tries to destroy those who are running for Jesus. The enemy doesn't want the weak or the dead either. He wants the strong and the beautiful. He wants the biggest fish; the dead can't be hooked. Although some of us are running a different race, we are all in the same waters, land, and skies. Some of us will die for nothing, and some will run for Jesus and receive eternal life."

*Behind every great man of God,*
*there is a great woman of God!*

ℱℬ

# The Faithful Church Member

Pastor Morgan was interested in hiring a new assistant pastor to help him with his ministry. He felt that it was too much work for him to do alone. He planned to pay a new assistant pastor a handsome salary to go out "door to door" as a missionary field worker while he worked in his office, praying and preparing for the weekly sermons.

One day, he informed all his church members as well as everyone in the entire county that he was seeking to hire an assistant pastor. There were several qualified pastors who applied, and he interviewed them all. Some had years of experience. Some were very educated. Some were renowned public speakers. All of them were very impressive men of God; it was a very difficult decision for Pastor Morgan to make, so he began to pray.

While Pastor Morgan was on his knees asking the Lord for an answer, the Lord spoke to him and told him to look out the window into the field. The church members owned a huge field and a garden. They also had a beautiful green lawn with shrubs and trees; it was all kept perfectly cut, trimmed, and tidy by a faithful church member who volunteered her time maintaining the grounds of the church. Today was an extremely hot day, and she was working very hard tending to the grounds.

She had been a very faithful church member for many years. As she worked, she sang beautiful, inspirational hymns. Sometimes people would walk by and watch her as she sang and hummed, worshiping God. Some people were curious and wanted to know why she chose such a nontraditional career. Some people would come into the field and share their problems with her or ask questions about God; she would always give them advice and pray for them.

This particular day, Pastor Morgan was watching the faithful church member from the window. "She gets up early and works alone in God's field without complaining. She willingly does the work that no one else wants to do. She doesn't mind getting dirty, and working in extreme hot weather. Even when she is tired, she sings and praises God," pastor Morgan thought.

After watching her for a few minutes, the pastor ran out to the field and approached her. Although the faithful church member was sweaty and dirty, Pastor Morgan gave her a big hug. "I've finally found the new pastor I was looking for. This new assistant pastor lives inside of me. Teach me to be more like you," said pastor Morgan, as he rolled up his sleeves and began working in the field beside the faithful church member.

## *Reflection*

I've been to many churches in my life. Many times I've seen women who actually run the church from the fields—from the "backgrounds." Although women are not always standing in the pulpits (and not always receiving the credit they deserve for the strength they provide), they are actually the "backbone" of the church. Behind every great man of God, there is a great woman (or two) of God!

Oh great woman of God, regardless of how you are seen in "man's eyes," God sees all that you do! Therefore, continue to be that faithful church member in secret, and God will reward you...before all men!

*Woman of God,*
*you are worth more*
*than money can buy!*

ℬ

# Worth a Penny

A well-known speaker started his motivational speech holding a penny in his hand. He asked his audience, "Who wants this penny?" No one said anything; everyone just looked around and at each other. Some of the audience members laughed. No one really appeared to take him seriously. Most of them shrugged him off as a joke. The speaker threw the penny into an empty container on a table in front of him.

The speaker added four more pennies to the container and asked the question, "Who wants these pennies?" Although no one answered, "Yes," he had captured the attention of the audience, and everyone became curious and patiently waited to hear the point the speaker was trying to make.

The speaker added nickels, dimes, quarters, and dollars to the container. He continued to add value to the container until it was overflowing with money. This time, before he could ask the question, everyone in the audience had their hand up, excitedly trying to express the fact that they wanted the container filled with money.

The speaker smiled and announced, "Just because you start out worthless in the eyes of people doesn't mean that you don't have value or that you will stay the same way people saw you in the beginning. Maybe you've been rejected, and maybe people laughed at you, because they only measure you by the material things that they can see. Don't allow people to discourage you. Wait patiently on the Lord. The Lord will keep bringing more and more to the table. He can fill any empty vessel. Of course, when people see that you are worth something in their eyes, they want you. But God wants you now! God wants the smallest amount, because God knows that every dollar starts out with 'just a penny.' Maybe people have told you that you're 'not worth a dime.' Maybe you've been stepped on like you're 'not worth a penny.' *You are precious in God's sight even if no one else wants you.*"

# Woman in the Mirror

A car's rear view mirror only gives you a distorted view. Objects in the rear view mirror may be closer than they appear. However, the view in front of a driver (the large window) shows a clearer picture. The large window in front of a driver allows us to see the true image.

However, sometimes we are too busy looking at our distorted, past situations to see the big, bright view ahead of us. The distorted view that we see causes us to choose the wrong paths, the wrong roads.

Listening to people who bring up our distorted past can also cause us to travel in the wrong direction. Although God is a forgiving God, we often seek man's approval, but man has a limited view. Man often has tunnel vision; therefore, we are often blind-sided by man's harsh judgments, causing us to run off our road into the deep ditches and sometimes into brick walls.

We must learn to see ourselves the way God sees us. God sees the woman in the mirror as a "beautiful woman of God!" Remember, you are the empowered woman of God. It is time for you to walk in your divine destiny! Now, go look in the mirror!

*While you're walking in God's divine destiny,*
*you may encounter some obstacles in your path*
*like friends who criticize you and tell you that*
*you are being punished by God. But, like Job,*
*you must continue to allow God to lead and guide!*

ℰℯ

# Things Are Rarely Like They Seem

The 73-year-old mother of a very close friend of mine fell down on the floor while cooking in her kitchen. The fall left a severe bruise at the top of her left breast area. She felt fine before the fall; she said that she felt "fit as a fiddle" and wouldn't normally go to see a doctor, but the bruised area was very sore.

She went to her family doctor and after examining her, he referred her to a radiologist for a mammogram. Much to everyone's surprise, the mammogram test result showed that she had a cancerous tumor in her left breast.

Of course, this result was shocking to her, but she had a steadfast faith in God. She whole-heartedly believed that *"all things work together for good to them that love God, to them who are the called according to His purpose."* (Rom. 8:28).

She went back to her family doctor, and he began explaining that she would need to be treated by a specialist, an oncologist. When the doctor came to explain the surgical procedure to her, she was smiling and praising God.

"Hallelujah and glory to God. It's such a wonderful day to be alive. Praise God; He is such a good God, Glory to His name," she happily praised.

The doctor noticed how calm and peaceful she was, and he said, "You are certainly a very strong woman. I've never met anyone who reacted to this type of diagnosis in this manner before."

As scheduled, she went into the hospital to have the cancerous tumor removed. The doctor said that the surgery seemed to have "went well."

She went to the doctor for a follow-up exam to see if all the cancerous cells were removed. If the test showed that there were still some cancerous cells left, she would either need chemotherapy or possibly another surgery. The test results showed that all the cancerous cells had been removed. She didn't need chemotherapy or any more surgeries.

During her follow-up visit to her doctor, he said to her, "I have never seen such faith in anyone before; your God must be real. I want to know more about Him." Well, of course, she was excited to hear what the doctor told her, and she invited him to her church. Her doctor became a faithful member of her church.

Now, whenever one of his patients is suffering from a terminal illness, he says to them, "I am going to refer you to a greater physician; He is a specialist in dealing with your illness. His name is Jesus, and I know that He can heal you."

This woman rarely went to the doctor. If she had not fallen, she wouldn't have had an opportunity to share her testimony. Her testimony healed the doctor who was spiritually dying and in desperate need of a cure from the Great Physician, Jesus.

This is a woman truly walking in her divine destiny!

JEREMIAH 17:14

*Heal me, O Lord, and I shall be healed; save me, and I shall be saved: For thou art my praise.*

More healing Scriptures:

- ✤ Isaiah 19:22
- ✤ Isaiah 30:26
- ✤ Isaiah 53:5
- ✤ Isaiah 57:17-18
- ✤ Genesis 20:17
- ✤ Psalm 147:3
- ✤ Acts 10:38

*Even the most distant dreams can be realized
with determination and patience,
regardless of the obstacles in front of you!*

৪৯

# Succeed!

How does a woman run in a marathon race without the use of her own legs? How did a poor little girl from the "backwoods" of Mississippi overcome seemingly impossible odds and become the world-renowned Oprah?

The answer: Intangible resources, they are your greatest resources. You can use these resources to get anything you want in life.

Your determination, talents, strength, love, and faith are some of your intangible resources. People perish without a vision. Even if everyone laughs at your dreams, you must be determined to follow your dreams. Your destiny is inside of you. All you really need to succeed is already inside you. God has planted seeds in you. These seeds are planted deep down inside of you in a dark place where you or no one else can see until they are cultivated, grow, and manifest themselves, becoming lights for you and others around you.

Your gifts and talents, your faith and determination, your experience and even your pain are already inside of you. You are already equipped with everything necessary to lead you to Jesus and develop a relationship with Him. Jesus will work a wonderful "seed thing" in your life. God can turn tragedy into triumph!

Years ago, when I first told people that I was going to become a storyteller, many of them laughed! Surely the ridicule was supposed to bring me to my senses, but it only made me stronger and more determined. When I didn't feel like getting up in the morning, I used that negative motivation to jump-start me into gear. God gave me a gift, and I'm going to use it!

The enemy is defeated, and I will have the victory, and so will you! No weapon formed against me or you shall prosper (Isa. 54:17)! I am, I can, I will succeed, and so will you! Years ago, my son and I lived in low-income project housing; we lived without a television, telephone, washer, dryer, car, bed, and other furniture. I didn't have things that people take for granted like a microwave or a radio. I lived in that project apartment for four years. I remember praying to God, asking Him to somehow give me a bed to sleep on. I was tired of sleeping on the floor. It was scorching hot in that project apartment, and my son and I didn't have an air conditioner or even a fan.

It wasn't just my financial situation that was so painful, but what hurt me the most is that I was afraid; I was absolutely terrified! I also felt very alone, and I didn't have a clue about how I was going to raise my son. I thought about it day and night. God had given me a child that I couldn't take care of. I prayed day and night, and I cried day and night. I didn't know whether I was coming or going.

Now, I'm laughing all the way to the bank! I made lemonade out of all my lemons. The enemy has only been a footstool for me; if I hadn't suffered, I wouldn't have anything to write about! If people hadn't hurt me, I wouldn't have any characters to write about!

There will be some people who will support your endeavors, but there will also be people who expect you to fail. Allow your supporters *and* your non-supporters to motivate and strengthen you. Ironically, your non-supporters can make you work harder than ever to achieve your goals. Maybe you're being ridiculed and tormented by the best spirit-breakers in your town. They will cause you *not* to "go to sleep at the wheel" of life while it's turning, because you'll want to stick around a while to prove to your adversaries that they were dead wrong!

Jesus wants to help you show your adversaries how wrong they are. He wants to show your adversaries how much He loves you. He wants to prepare a table for you in the presence of your enemies. He wants everyone to know that you are His beautiful daughter, a divine creation.

Jesus wants to give you the garment of praise for the spirit of heaviness, beauty for your ashes, and the oil of glory for your mourning (see Isa. 61:3). Always keep God's word in your heart. Jesus wants to stake a claim over your life, and He will never disown you like men of this world.

If I had known, years ago, about the value of my redemption, I would have run to Jesus. Do you know the value of your redemption? When you know the value of your redemption, you don't wait, but you run without hesitation—you immediately run to Jesus and thank Him without ceasing. However, if you're depending on the validation of men, you'll never know the true value of your life. Don't give up. Your success is not determined by others. If God is for you, no man can be against you. God will make your enemies your footstool (Matt. 22:44).

Stay steadfast in prayer; be faithful and loving. Remember to pray for those who hurt you. You will fulfill your dreams. All you need is already inside of you. It's time to walk in your divine destiny!

*I heard Bishop T.D. Jakes preach
about a woman whose husband
always threatened to leave her. The
following sermon/story is not verbatim;
however, it is an accurate recollection.*

৳৯

# When He Leaves...

A woman's husband threatened day in and day out, "I'm leaving you." Therefore, in an effort to please him and keep him, the woman changed her hair; she constantly changed the style and the color. She permed her hair; sometimes she would cut it; other times, she would let it grow. She would get her nails manicured and sculptured. She would lose weight when her husband complained that she was too fat, and she would gain weight when her husband complained that she was too skinny—but he still threatened to leave her.

She tried to give her husband all the things that he needed and wanted. The thought of her husband leaving traumatized her; it caused her to have headaches and many sleepless nights.

Finally, her husband left her. At first, she was devastated. She cried out to God, "Please, God, help me. I feel lost and alone!" However, as time passed, she began to realize that her husband's threats were like shackles. For years, she was bound by the fear of him leaving. Now that he was finally gone, he wasn't able to control or imprison her with the fear of him leaving anymore.

"Now I can fix up the office room and make it a guest room. I've always wanted to do that..." she said to herself. After she finished remodeling, she decided to join a book club. Before her husband left, she could not invite girlfriends over to sit and talk.

She slowly began to find herself. She began to dress the way that she always wanted to dress. Before her husband left, she had to wear the same old dresses. Because she began to feel happier, she was able to get a better job. Before he left, her husband only allowed her to work part-time, and she had to be back home by 3 P.M. to cook him hot meals. She wasn't able to go back out of the house or talk on the telephone for the rest of the night.

After he left, she joined an aerobics class and took some computer classes. She even went on a cruise with some of her church girlfriends. One Sunday, a church member asked her, "Are you sad these days...that your husband left you?"

The woman replied, "Yes, I am sad about one thing...about all the years I wasted worrying and fearing. I regret that I lost so many years to fear; I wish that he had left me years ago, the very minute he threatened to leave!"

Regardless of what others may think, this woman is truly a woman—now—living her divine destiny!

### *Personal Feelings*

When he leaves, you're still not alone! You may find that you have become finally free from a situation that has kept you bound for a long time. Pray and write down your feelings—about the story or about a similar situation.

Even if you feel angry or resentful about past situations that have kept you bound, express your inner feelings this is the first step toward healing.

### *Scripture Analogies*

There are Scriptures that will heal and strengthen you. In fact, God has given you a special word for comfort and healing. Please pray first; then, read these Scriptures, writing your feelings as they become clear.

PHILIPPIANS 4:13

*I can do all things through Christ which strengtheneth me.*

<br>

JOHN 14:18

*I will not leave you comfortless: I will come to you.*

(Even when it appears as though the whole world has left you, God will never leave you nor forsake you.)

<br>

PSALM 46:1-3

*God is our refuge and strength, a very present help in trouble. Therefore will not we fear, though the earth be removed, and though the mountains be carried into the midst of the sea; Though the waters thereof roar and be troubled, though the mountains shake with the swelling thereof.*

<br>

2 TIMOTHY 1:7

*For God hath not given us the spirit of fear; but of power, and of love, and of a sound mind.*

<br>

PSALM 56:11

*In God have I put my trust: I will not be afraid what man can do unto me.*

_____

_____

Now, think of a time when God has delivered you from something painful (anything), or think of something good that God has done in your life.

_____

_____

_____

_____

Write the things that you must do in order to continue to walk in faith and please God.

_____

_____

_____

_____

Please remember that your past pain will be a testimony for someone else who is presently suffering from a similar situation. You will glorify God when you share your testimony.

*Allow God to lead and guide you; God*
*may instruct you to "miss" the appointment!*

႘ஐ

# The Appointment

There was once a husband and a wife who were having troubles in their marriage. They had been married for 20 years, but they were living together like strangers. They were so busy with their separate careers and their separate lives…that they rarely spent time together. They spent less time together with each passing day.

Finally, they both agreed that a divorce might be the answer. They scheduled appointments with two separate attorneys. They also owned two separate cars, but the wife had recently been in a car accident, and her car was being repaired.

On the day of his wife's appointment, her husband had to drive her to the attorney's office. It was rare for them to be in the same car together. He opened the car door for her.

"You sure look nice today. Is that a new dress?" the husband asked his wife.

"No, but it's a dress that you probably haven't had a chance to see. You look very nice, yourself. Is that a new suit?" the wife asked her husband.

"No, it's a suit that you probably haven't had a chance to see," replied her husband.

While they were driving, they were listening to the radio and singing along with the songs.

"That song sure brings back memories," said the husband.

"Yes, they are playing our favorite songs," said the wife.

"Are you hungry?" asked the husband.

"Yes, we rarely have time for breakfast. It would certainly be nice to eat breakfast together," said the wife.

While eating a delicious breakfast, they talked about the good years that they had shared together. They even laughed and talked about some of the mistakes they made when they were first married.

He gazed into her eyes for the first time in years.

"You have the most beautiful smile in the world, and your eyes are dancing," said the husband.

She began to remember why she fell in love with him years ago. She fell in love with him for several reasons. One reason was because he always paid attention to and appreciated little things about her.

"Lets go for a walk; we have time," suggested the husband.

"Sure, we haven't taken a walk together in ages. It's such a beautiful day; yes, let's go for a walk," agreed the wife.

They talked, held hands, and from time to time hugged each other closely while walking.

"You know, we don't have to keep our appointment," mentioned the husband lovingly.

"You know, we have become so busy and our lives have become so complicated that we actually had to schedule an appointment in order to have time for each other. (laughing) This used to be called 'dating,'" said the wife.

They both laughed and held each other closely.

"Maybe we should schedule appointments more often," suggested the husband.

"Yes, let's get together again soon," replied the wife.

# The Stubborn Mule

A man owned an old mule that had given him years of service and companionship. The mule went everywhere that his master went. This mule was more valuable to him than all the other mules, because when his master really needed some work to be done, the mule would always do whatever was necessary to get the job done. The mule was stubborn in a good way, because no matter how tired he was, he would never give up until the job was done. Regardless of the amount of work his master gave him, the mule would not stop until he finished the job that he was told to do.

One day, while following his master, the mule fell into a big well. It was an extremely deep well. The mule's master knew that it would be very difficult to get his mule out. While his master grieved over the mule being lost in the deep well, his friends decided that they would help him by burying the mule inside the well. His friends began to shovel dirt into the well.

When the mule saw that people were shoveling dirt into the well to bury him, he became more determined than ever to get out of his terrible trouble. When they shoveled dirt down the well, it would fall on top of the mule's head and back. He decided to shake off the dirt, because he was determined that he was not going to die. He did this repeatedly. Each time someone would shovel dirt on top of him, he would shake the dirt off. The mule noticed that he had shaken the dirt off into a pile just big enough for him to step his two front legs on top of. He continued to shake off dirt that was intended to bury him. Each time, he'd shake the dirt off and step on top of the dirt. He did this until he was able to make steps high enough to lead him out of the well.

The mule climbed out of the well and began faithfully serving his master again.

*Like the mule, we must understand that the enemy is our footstool. Each time things that are meant to bury us come our way, we must shake off the dirt and step on top of it so that we can climb out of our deep well and faithfully begin serving our Master again.*

*It is good to know God's plan…*
*so that we don't get in His way!*

೪ಎ

# God's Plan

A man found a cocoon of an emperor moth. He took it home so that he could watch the moth emerge from the cocoon.

On the day a small opening appeared, he sat and watched the moth for several hours as it struggled to force its body through that little hole. Then it seemed to stop making any progress. It appeared as if it had gotten as far as it could, and it could go no farther. It seemed to be stuck. Then the man, in his kindness, decided to help the moth, so he took a pair of scissors and snipped off the remaining bit of the cocoon.

The moth emerged easily. But it had a swollen body and small, shriveled wings. The man continued to watch the moth because he expected that at any moment the wings would enlarge and expand be able to support the body, which would contract in time. Neither happened! In fact, the little moth spent the rest of its life crawling with a swollen body and shriveled wings. It never was able to fly.

What the man in his kindness and haste did not understand was that the restricting cocoon and the struggle required for the moth to get through the tiny opening were God's way of forcing fluid from the body of the moth into its wings so that it would be ready for flight once it achieved its freedom from the cocoon. Freedom and flight would only come after the struggle. By depriving the moth of a struggle, the man deprived the moth of health.

Sometimes, struggles are exactly what we need in our life. If God allowed us to go through life without any obstacles, He would cripple us. We would not be as strong as we could be. How true this is!

How many times have we wanted to take the quick way out of struggles and difficulties, to take those scissors and snip off the remaining bits in an attempt to be free. We need to remember that our loving Father will never give us more than we can bear, and through our trials and struggles, we are strengthened as gold is refined in the fire.

*May we never let the things we can't have, or don't have, or shouldn't have, spoil our enjoyment of the things we do have and can have. Don't focus on the things you **don't** have, enjoy each moment of every day God has given you.*

*This is the day which the Lord hath made; We will rejoice and be glad in it* (Ps. 118:24).

*Laughter is good medicine!*

℘

# Don't Mess With Grandma!

An elderly Florida lady did her shopping, and upon returning to her car found four males in the act of leaving with her vehicle. She dropped her shopping bags and pulled out her handgun. Then she began to scream at the top of her voice, "I have a gun, and I know how to use it! Get out of the car!"

The four men didn't wait for a second invitation. They got out and ran like mad! The lady, somewhat shaken, then proceeded to load her shopping bags into the back of the car and got into the driver's seat. She was so shaken that she could not get her key into the ignition. She tried and tried; then, it dawned on her why.

A few minutes later, she found her own car parked four or five spaces farther down the row. She loaded her bags into the car and drove to the police station. The sergeant, to whom she told the whole story, couldn't stop laughing.

He pointed to the other end of the counter where four men were reporting a car jacking by a mad, elderly woman described as white, less than 5 feet tall, glasses, curly white hair, and carrying a large hand-gun. No charges were filed.

*If you're going to have a "senior moment," make it a memorable one!*

# A Good Man Is Hard to Find

For years Friday nights for us (my two girlfriends and I) was "girls' night out." We would get together and either go to strip clubs or just sit and talk about the men in our lives, about how well endowed they were (or not).

Friday nights were always fun, but no matter how much fun we had, at the end of the night, the three of us departed each other with an empty feeling; we just never admitted it to one another. The three of us were unmarried, but we were all looking for a "good man." However, a good man seemed hard to find. We were tired of meeting men who lived in the basement with their "mama," men who were broke or stingy, and men who were "all talk and no action."

The difference this Friday was that I had an announcement to make. Last Sunday morning, I gave my life to Christ. It was time for me to tell my best friends about my new-found relationship with Christ.

When Friday night came, I was a little nervous at first. But we were the best of girlfriends, and we didn't keep anything from each other. Also, if I was going to begin witnessing for Christ, I had to become bold—not shy. This Friday, it was my turn to entertain. I made it clear to them before they came over that we wouldn't be watching any x-rated movies or getting high. I told them that we were just going to talk.

"Last Sunday, I became a Christian, and I'm not going to be sexually active anymore. No more sex in the city or the country for me until I'm married. Now, I'm committed to Christ. I belong to God, mind, body, and spirit! If you're interested in staying tonight and learning more about Christ, please stay, and we can talk. If either of you aren't interested and want to leave, I understand," I said to my girlfriends.

They both stayed, and the three of us talked. "Are you sick? Do you have cancer?" they asked. I told them that I felt better than ever. They wanted to know how I could "just jump up and make such a big life-changing decision."

I answered, "We've been playing Russian roulette with our lives for years, sleeping around with men. It only takes one bullet. We might use protection in the beginning, but after we think we know the guy, we don't use it anymore. For years, we've put our trust and confidence in men, only to be disappointed in the end. I don't want to keep living this way."

My girlfriends had lots of questions. "Aren't you afraid?" "Won't you miss your old life?" "Are you going to quit your job as a stripper?" they asked.

I answered, "I'm going to take one day at a time. I've already taken the biggest step. I've surrendered my life to Christ, and I'm not going to turn back."

They asked, "Well, there is no way I could go without having sex." "Won't you miss having sex?"

I replied confidently, "I've learned that sex is a trap, a trick of the enemy...No matter how good a man is in bed, it's only temporary satisfaction. After each encounter, I found that I was still unfulfilled and 'waiting to exhale.' Sin was weighing me down. I could never get high enough or the sexual pleasure wasn't long enough. Now, I'm seeking lasting peace and comfort; I want lasting joy and love. I want to be complete, and I know that God is the only true source."

I continued to explain to them that I wanted to have security and protection in my life and that I wanted to have peace in my heart before I go to bed at night. I told them that I believe that there are some things that only God can give.

"There may be some good men out there, but they are few and far in between. Therefore, a good man is hard to find if you're trying to find one on your own. In order to get a good man, you must allow God to lead and guide you. God will not only get a man ready for you, but He will also get you ready for the man whom He has chosen for you! I truly believe this with all my heart!" I said.

I thought that I would lose my two girlfriends, but it turned out that I had set an example that they wanted to follow. Now on Friday nights, we still get together, but we talk about godly matters, and we sing and praise God. The three of us are committed to God and are determined to wait until God sends us a good man. We realize that without God's guidance, a good man is hard to find.

*Nicodemus asked, "What does it mean to be born again?"* (see John 3:4-16)

Our body is a temple. When we receive Christ, the old woman or man (inside of us) dies, but the spirit of Jesus comes and creates a new life inside of us. God gives us a new spirit, a life of love. We become filled with His Spirit, and there is no more room for the old woman or man inside our temple. (See 2 Corinthians 5:17.)

*So many women struggle to try to lose weight. If you've tried to lose weight, and you can't seem to do it on your own, it's time to try God. Because with God, all things are possible!*

૪๑

# With God, All Things Are Possible!

It was career day, and each student had to stand up and tell the class what they planned to become in life and how they planned to achieve their goals when they grew up. Carla's teacher told the class to be honest and serious about their career goals, because she wanted to make sure that their goals were realistic. When it was Carla's turn, she stood up excitedly and said, "I want to become a beautiful fashion model."

Carla didn't get an opportunity to tell her high school friends how she planned to achieve her goal, because her classmates interrupted her with laughter and ugly comments. They said, "That's impossible, because you're too fat; you can't be serious." Even Carla's teacher said, "You have plenty of time, Carla, and you might change your mind, later." But Carla's biggest surprise came at the end of the school day, when her best friend said, "Carla, you have to be realistic. There are lots of jobs that you will be able to do, but you could never become a fashion model unless you lose a lot of weight."

Carla's feelings were hurt, and she tried to put the whole horrible day behind her. Nevertheless, some of the children wouldn't let her forget about it. She was teased all through high school. Carla thought about dropping out of school, but deep down inside she was not a quitter. Also, she knew that the Lord would not approve of her dropping out of school. Carla truly loved the Lord. She was a very humble and sincere Christian and did not do anything without asking the Lord about it first. Carla prayed about her career goals and the Lord spoke to her heart, telling her that with Him, all things are possible. The Lord also told her that if she trusted in Him that He would surely direct her path and give her the desires of her heart.

After graduating high school, Carla felt that she desperately needed a change from her small town surroundings, so she prayed about it, and the Lord spoke to her heart and told her to move to New York City. It was a big, beautiful place. With God's help, she registered for classes at a university and met many new friends; she loved school and her new friends. Although she wasn't confronted daily with her weight problem, she decided that she would like to try to lose some weight anyway. Again, she prayed about the idea, and the Lord approved the idea. She signed up for a Weight Watchers® program with the help of the Lord.

The officials and directors at the program recognized that she was different. Everyone in the program had experienced a weight problem at one time or another; therefore, no one physically "stood out in the crowd," but Carla had something different on the *inside*. She had a special, humble, sincere, dedicated spirit, and some marketing directors approached her and asked her if she wanted to become their new "role model" and spokesperson.

Carla was very excited, but she did not make a decision before first praying about it. As usual, Jesus was directing her path. He confirmed to her that she was making the right decision. She accepted their offer and began appearing on television commercials and in magazine articles. Everyone fell in love with her warm and friendly personality. She became a huge success. Several agents and television personalities contacted her, asking her if she could promote other products. Of course, Carla never made a move without the Lord's approval. With the help of the Lord, Carla soon became a model for a leading cosmetic company as well as a leading shoe corporation and perfume company. Again, with the help of the Lord,

Carla eventually formed her own designer clothing line and modeled her clothes around the world.

Carla became a renowned fashion model and motivational speaker. Years later, at her class reunion, Carla had to stand up and tell her former classmates if she had fulfilled her childhood dreams and how she did it. This time around, everyone recognized her as a celebrity, and no one interrupted her. Carla stood up and said, "My name is Carla Thomas, and being overweight did not stop me from fulfilling my childhood career aspirations. I achieved the impossible with the help of the Lord! With God, all things are possible! *With God, all things are possible.*"

*Man looks at the outer appearance, but God looks at the heart.*

*Does your husband have a secret? This true story exposes a sensitive situation and raises many questions that are difficult to answer without God's guidance.*

ℰ

# My Husband's Secret

Our lives seemed perfect. My husband (a minister) and I had three children, a beautiful home, and we both had wonderful parents. My husband's father had also been a minister. One day, "out of the blue," my husband told me that he was gay. I just couldn't believe it!

It was like a tornado or a hurricane came and blew away our beautiful lives. Well, I wish that it had been just that simple. It's extremely difficult to explain. My husband told me that he had been sleeping with a man for the past two years.

We weren't sexually active and hadn't been for a while, but he had explained to me years ago that it was because he was "just so spiritually involved" with God and the church...that it totally consumed him. However, he constantly told me that he loved our children and me and that his involvement with the church only heightened his love and faithfulness to us, his family.

We lived in a small town and were leaders of a wonderful community church. Together we had counseled many couples about adultery, but never had I encountered anything like this situation.

I had so many questions. "Maybe we could receive some sort of marriage counseling," I thought, but when I asked my husband about it, he said that it wouldn't help. He said that he had been born gay but that he had fought his feelings and hid the fact for all these years.

Now, he said that he must come "out of the" closet in order to be "free." He also said that he had to tell me, because his gay lover insisted, or he would tell everyone about their relationship. My husband began to talk about the details of their sexual relationship which made me angry. My oldest daughter told me about a video by "R. Kelly" involving a preacher coming out of the closet. I explained to her that this wasn't a video: This was real life!

I asked my husband, "Since you're so willing to come out of the closet and share all the details of your gay sex life, tell me how could it be possible? You and I created three children together." He said that he had "learned" to act like a heterosexual many years ago but that he was always a homosexual. All these years, he was actually "living a lie." "I learned to play the role," he said. But how could he say that he ever loved me when he was gay and didn't know how to truly love any woman? How could he do this to me?

I tried to put aside my feelings and think about our children. "What about our children? Can't you stop what you're doing just for the children's sake?" I asked. But he insisted that he had lived all these years for the sake of others. "I knew that my father would disown me, so I pretended to be the kind of man he wanted me to be. I lived for him for most of my life. Now my father is finally dead. Years ago, when I married you, I honestly tried to be the man you needed, wanted, and deserved, but no matter how hard I tried, I wasn't happy; it wasn't the 'real' me."

There was no explanation good enough for me. Nothing he said to me made any sense at all. I had always known that my husband wasn't one to chase women. He only had one other girlfriend before me, but I thought that meant he was a good catch! I thought it meant that he was a faithful "man of God!"

I had a few girlfriends who had husbands who loved to chase women and continued to do so even after they were married. Since my husband wasn't a womanizer, I thought that I was blessed.

I don't claim to be "street smart," but I don't consider myself naive either. Through my dealings in the church, I've met all kinds of people, and I always pictured a homosexual man to be a man who acts feminine. Obviously, I had a lot to learn, because my husband was a big, strong, burly man with a deep voice and manly mannerisms.

At first, I wasn't convinced that he wasn't leaving me for another woman. I still can't believe that he's gay. I think that I would be able to deal with the idea of having a homosexual son or a lesbian daughter; it would be such a different situation, but I just can't deal with my husband being gay.

I wonder if he's going to start walking around wearing women's clothing, or will he be a masculine homosexual. I wonder, "Which one of them will play the woman's role, or do they even have gender roles? Do they get up in the morning and choose which one they want to be for that day?" I don't think that I'll ever get over this!

I remember watching Oprah and seeing a woman whose husband told her that he wanted a sex change. He had the sex change and the couple stayed married, even after he became a woman. He was wearing women's clothes before he had the surgery; then, he actually became a transsexual, and they (amazingly) stayed together.

I'd also seen on another television show how some men in prison would have sexual relationships with men; then get out of prison and have sexual relationships with their wives, who had no clue that their husbands lived homosexual lives while they were incarcerated. Some of them called it living on the "down-low." Even when their wives found out, they stayed with their husbands.

I, on the other hand, just couldn't do it. There was no way that I was going to stay married to my gay husband. He wanted to be free anyway. He wanted to go and live with his gay lover.

I read about men who go to church "only to hide" their homosexuality behind the church. These gay men are preaching from the pulpits and singing in choirs. The article talked about gay lovers (in the closet) who live together (pretending to be platonic friends), while they confess that Christ has saved them; they go to church, only to hide behind the church and God.

I thought about all the people who had been saved during my husband's ministry. "What would they think now? What would they do now?" I thought about all the sermons and all the baptisms. He had married several couples. I wondered what would make a man who appeared to love God throw away everything that he worked for so many years.

Well, I don't have all those answers, but I had to share my story, because it's a true story, and there are women out there, right now, who are experiencing my pain.

My husband and I eventually got a divorce; we dissolved our marriage, but the damage and destruction wasn't dissolved as easily. He went to live with his gay lover, and he has started a gay ministry—a church filled with men who confess that they are gay Christians. My husband told me that he was going to marry his partner and that they were going to adopt children. Recently, my husband's lover was diagnosed with full-blown AIDS.

My children and I are still devastated! I continue to pray daily for my healing! I believe that God is a healer and a deliverer for those who diligently seek Him!

Sincerely,
*A Woman of Divine Destiny*

### *Grandma Joy's P.S.*

The following Scripture is helpful to memorize and hide in your heart when situations seem too hard to handle. *We are troubled on every side, yet not distressed; we are perplexed, but not in despair; Persecuted, but not forsaken; cast down, but not destroyed* (2 Cor. 4:8-9).

*There are still some good men in this world!*
*Part of being a Christian is being a witness.*
*This story will help you explain God's*
*redemption to all the people you meet! Read*
*this story and go out and tell everyone*
*you meet that they've been set free!*

ℬℛ

# Been Set Free

A young pastor stood before his congregation to deliver his first sermon. He held up an empty birdcage and placed it on a table. Eyebrows were raised as curious church members waited to hear the young preacher. The preacher explained:

This morning, I was walking through the park meditating, and I saw a little boy holding this birdcage with three little birds inside of it. The birds were hungry and weak; they were shivering from fright.

I asked the boy, "What are you going to do with those birds?" He replied, "I'm going to have some fun with them. I'm going to pluck their feathers and make 'em mad and fight each other. I'm going to starve them—and then when I'm finished having fun, I'm going to feed them to the cats."

I asked, "How much would you sell them for?" The boy replied, "Mister, I don't think you want these birds. These birds are ugly and dirty. They can't fly and they can't even sing."

"Are they tainted?" I asked. "What does taint mean?" the boy asked. "It means that they are stained, unclean," I replied.

Then I pulled out a $10 bill and offered it to him. The boy snatched the money out of my hand and ran away as fast as he could, leaving behind the birds in the cage.

Well, years ago, a similar transaction occurred between satan and Jesus. Satan had a locked cage filled with helpless sparrows—people like you and me. He showed us how to create weapons of mass destruction, guns, and drugs, and put hate in our hearts for each other. He was torturing us with diseases and afflictions. He planned to kill us when he finished playing tricks and games with our lives; he was going to take us to an eternal lake of fire—with him, forever.

But, before he could carry out all his plans, Jesus came and asked, "How much for those sparrows?" The devil laughed and said, "You don't want these ugly, tainted sparrows. They can't fly. They can't even sing."

Jesus asked again, "What is the price?"

Satan replied, "Ha! You want these birds? They will crucify you. They will spit on you and drive nails in your hands. They will make you a crown of thorns and scourge—beat and whip—you at the pillar. They will even make you carry your own cross. Who would try to save these treacherous wretches? They will be with me and burn forever in the lake of fire. Ha! They are lost forever!

But, if you are willing to pay with your life...if you are willing to leave your glorious seat in Heaven and live here on earth as a regular human being—not as a spirit, only as a man, subject to all temptations by me...if you will suffer more than any man on earth has ever suffered and come without a crown, but as a humble servant—as humble as a little lamb...if you will allow me to come to you and tempt you every chance I get, just like I do with all other men here on earth...hey, if you are who you claim you are, it won't matter anyway...but I must have the opportunity to tempt you. If you'll agree to all these things, I'll set them free. The rest of your pain, your most horrible death, will come from their hands, anyway. They will crucify you. That's their passion, and they can't wait to do it. Ha! These sparrows will never change. They will never love you! But just for the pleasure of seeing them mock you, they are yours!" said satan.

"Done," said Jesus.

And Jesus lovingly took the cage with the helpless sparrows inside, and He opened the door of the cage and set us all free. As each one of us flew out of the cage, Jesus touched us, and we were healed and filled with His Spirit. He prayed for each one of us individually. He told us that He loved us and that we should love Him and trust Him and most of all, He said that we should always *love one another*. He said, "I must go, but I promise to be back. I will prepare a place for you in Heaven, and you will not have to go with satan, because I am the redeemer; I came to pay the price for your salvation. You have been set free forever because God the Father loves you.

"Please don't let satan trick you and catch you in his snare. He's a thief, but you are mine. Now fly away high and soar like an eagle because I paid the price and you've been set free."

*Laughter is good medicine!*

ക

# Just a Weeeee Bit

An extraordinarily handsome man decided he had the responsibility to marry the perfect woman so they could produce beautiful children beyond comparison.

With that as his mission he began searching for the perfect woman.

Shortly thereafter he met a farmer who had three stunning, gorgeous daughters who positively took his breath away. So he explained his mission to the farmer, asking for permission to marry one of them.

The farmer simply replied, "They're lookin' to get married, so you came to the right place. Look 'em over and pick the one you want."

The man took the first daughter on a date and the next day the farmer asked for the man's opinion.

"Well," said the man, "she's just a weeeee bit, not that you can hardly notice…pigeon-toed."

The farmer nodded and suggested the man date one of the other girls; so the man went out with the second daughter.

The next day the farmer again asked how things went.

"Well," the man replied, "she's just a weeeee bit, not that you can hardly tell…cross-eyed."

The farmer nodded and suggested he date the third girl to see if things might be better. So he did.

The next morning the man rushed in exclaiming, "She's perfect, just perfect. She's the one I want to marry."

So they were wed right away. Months later the baby was born. When the man visited the nursery he was horrified: the baby was ugly—not what the young man expected…He rushed to his father-in-law asking how such a thing could happen considering the beauty of the parents.

"Well," explained the farmer, "she was just a weeeee bit, not that you could hardly tell…pregnant when you met her."

*We are all lifetime learners.*

৪৯

# A Time to Learn

She had no children, no real friends; she had lots of family who never visited her or showed her any kind of love while she was alive. She was labeled "the black sheep" of the family because she had made lots of mistakes and because she was considered "unlearned." She was the only one in the family who never graduated high school, and she didn't have a prestigious career or livelihood like all her brothers and sisters. Although she was the outcast, the others (her brothers and sisters) weren't close to each other either.

She had no insurance; therefore, family members were contacted to see if they could raise money for the cost of her burial. Initially, over the telephone, her brothers and sisters were not interested in attending her funeral, but they willingly consented to help with the burial costs. They were ashamed of her and didn't want anyone to know that she was a relative.

On her deathbed, she wrote a letter, left it with the funeral director, and requested that it be read to all her family members. This is what the letter said:

## A Time to Learn

*It's okay if no one grieves for me, because it's not a time to grieve, it is a time to learn. In my life I've made lots of mistakes, but before I died I learned some things. The greatest thing I learned was to give my life to Christ. I learned to allow God to forgive me of my sins. I learned to forgive others, and I learned to ask for forgiveness.*

*By the time you read this letter, I'll be on the other side. From my death, I hope that you all learn to love each other—now—while you are all breathing, learn to forgive and ask for forgiveness.*

*Please come to my funeral, but don't come for me. Please come and be united, all of you, and learn from my death. Learn that life is short, and we have to give people their flowers while they are living. Learn not to judge people, but pray for them while they are living. Learn to be united as brothers and sisters in Christ.*

*I gave my life to Christ. From my death, learn to give your lives to Christ too. Don't wait until it's too late—learn now to give unconditional love to those who are hard to love.*

*You don't need to grieve for me, because I am not labeled a black sheep anymore. My Father God has given me a new name and a new life in heaven. Now, from my life and my death, you must learn about life's biggest lesson: Learn, while all of you are still living, to love each other with all your heart, the way Christ loves you.*

*Love,*

*The Learned Sister of Christ*

*Don't you know...that*
*laughter is good medicine?*
*Don't you know...that God*
*will make the enemy your footstool?*

ℱℨ

# Don't You Know?

There was a Christian lady who lived next door to an atheist. Everyday when the lady prayed, the atheist guy could hear her. He thought to himself, "She sure is crazy. Praying all the time like that. Doesn't she know there isn't a God?"

Many times while she was praying, he would go to her house and harass her, saying, "Lady, why do you pray all the time? Don't you know that there is no God?" But she kept on praying.

One day, she ran out of groceries. As usual, she was praying to the Lord, explaining her situation and thanking Him for what He was going do. As usual, the atheist heard her praying and thought to himself. "Humph...I'll fix her."

He went to the grocery store, bought a whole bunch of groceries, took them to her house, dropped them off on the front porch, rang the doorbell, and then hid in the bushes to see what she would do. When she opened the door and saw the groceries, she began to praise the Lord with all her heart, jumping, singing, and shouting everywhere!

The atheist jumped out of the bushes and told her, "You old crazy lady, God didn't buy you those groceries, I bought those groceries! Here's the receipt!"

Well, she broke out and started running down the street, shouting and praising the Lord. When he finally caught up with her, he asked what her problem was. She said, "I knew the Lord would provide me with some groceries, but I didn't know He was gonna make the devil pay for them!"

*Always remember that God will bless you in ways you least expect. God can use people you least expect to bless you. Just keep on shouting and praising the Lord! The Lord will always bless you!*

*If you have an "Uncle Willie"*
*in your life now or in your past,*
*know that God can help and heal.*

❦

# I'm Sorry...

Uncle Willie got drunk every Friday night, and stayed drunk until it was time for him to go back to work on Monday. None of us knew it back then, but he had molested three generations of women in our family. He had molested my mother, my cousin, my niece, and me.

We were all too embarrassed and ashamed to talk about it. Also, none of his victims (including me) knew that he had other victims in our family. We never realized that "speaking out" saves others from abuse.

I remember "way back" when I was only 4 years old when Uncle Willie always giving us (my sister, other children in the neighborhood, and me) candy and money. All the children used to love to come over to play with Uncle Willie. We all saw him as "just a big kid." He was so much fun, because he played with us just like a child.

In the beginning, he was the best uncle in the world! But after months of spoiling us with candy and money, he started doing something to me that I was too young to understand. "Come sit on Uncle Willie's lap, and I'll bounce you off my knee," he'd say. Then, before I knew it, he had his hands up my dress, and I was too afraid and confused to do or say anything.

If he thought, though, that I might have the courage to speak out, he'd say, "They've all seen you run to sit on my lap many times before. No one will believe you anyway if you try to tell someone what I'm doing. They'll just say that you're a liar, because everybody loves to sit on Uncle Willie's lap."

I was too ashamed and embarrassed to tell anyone, because I had been sitting on Uncle Willie's lap long before he began to molest me. I was too young to communicate the fact that I was being manipulated and deceived by a grown man. I felt dirty and confused, and I never wanted to sit on his lap, ever again. So I thought that the abuse would stop! I thought that it would all end if I never sat on Uncle Willie's lap again!

However, it wasn't over! One day, my grandmother left Uncle Willie to baby-sit my sister and me. While my sister was outside playing, he followed me into the bathroom and raped me; there was blood all over the bathroom. He said that if I screamed, everyone would tease me and call me nasty names. Uncle Willie kept saying, "You want me to keep it a secret, don't you? You don't want anyone to find out what you've been doing, do you?"

It was a nightmare that I thought would never end. I was about 7 years old when I finally got the courage to try telling someone. I decided to tell his girlfriend, Emma. She seemed so much stronger than everybody else; she was always cursing Uncle Willie out about something. She stood up to him like no one else dared to. Uncle Willie had been married four times, and Emma was soon to be number five.

My sister and I lived with our grandmother. She loved us, but she loved her son (Uncle Willie) even more. He was her pride and joy. In grandma's eyes, Uncle Willie could do no wrong. Therefore, I decided that it would be better to tell his soon-to-be fifth wife, Aunt Emma, about the abuse instead of telling grandma.

I asked Aunt Emma to come into a room with me, alone, and I told her that Uncle Willie had hurt me "down there." I did not expect her to react the way she reacted. She grabbed me and shook me real hard and said, "He was telling the truth the whole time. You *are* a fast little girl. He told me that you had been touching him, and he told you to stop. You are a bad little girl, and I'm going to tell your grandmother!"

At that point, I wished that I had kept my mouth shut, because now I was in serious trouble. Uncle Willie said that no one would believe me. Well, he was right. At that time, I kept thinking, "Why did I have to tell it? I should have kept my big mouth shut! It didn't do any good to tell anyone. It seemed to only make things worse."

Ever since I can remember, Uncle Willie had claimed to be a preacher, a devoted man of God, even though he got drunk on weekends. I'm 40 years old now and until this day, I can say that Uncle Willie is the biggest con-artist I've ever met in my life! I've never known a better whoremonger, liar, or thief. But what I didn't understand when I was 4 years old is that there was a demon spirit, a principality that lived inside Uncle Willie.

Well, Aunt Emma told grandma and Uncle Willie, and they all got together and said that I was a liar, and I needed prayer. My grandma told Uncle Willie to pray for me. He did. He laid his hands on my forehead and asked God to forgive me for lies that I told. His girlfriend said that she forgave me but that I needed to pray and ask God for forgiveness.

"Child, you know better than to lie on your Uncle Willie, good as he's been to you. I don't know how you can fix yo' mouth to tell such lies about Willie Junior. The devil must have gotten into you! Willie pays the bills round here, and you gone lie on him like that! Now, you need to go tell yo' Uncle Willie that you sorry and stop telling lies. Now, I don't want to hear no more about that kind of talk."

"The devil is just busy; that's all, and I forgive her. I have a great call, a great mission to be used by God, and that's why the devil wants to try to stop me," said Uncle Willie.

I grew up knowing that Uncle Willie was a pedophile, but I just kept it to myself. As soon as I graduated, I left home and moved out-of-state to go to college. Yet, there was something in me that wouldn't allow me to rest. In college, I took certain courses like psychology and American literature that caused me to think about my past and my womanhood. I thought that I had buried my pain, but my burden wouldn't go away. I prayed daily for healing.

Then it happened. Uncle Willie died. By the time Uncle Willie died, *he had all the females in our family angry with one another.* He had literally divided up our family, and none of the women in our family spoke to each other.

There weren't many people at the funeral. Among the few bereaved were his five wives and their children, along with my mother, my sister's daughter, and me—the one who publicly stated the fact that I hated Uncle Willie and that I was glad he died. Before the funeral, I said to myself, "I'm only going to the funeral to 'celebrate' the death of Uncle Willie."

My mother and I hadn't talked to each other in ten years. For over a decade, I resented the fact that she didn't raise me. She left me with my grandmother and with Uncle Willie. At this time, my sister and my grandmother were deceased. My grandmother died of a broken heart, and my sister died of unknown causes.

After Uncle Willie's funeral was over, Aunt Emma persuaded me to come over to grandma's house so that she could talk to me. I did; I went over to that house. It brought back all the memories. Every room was filled with heartache and pain, and I couldn't contain myself; I just burst out in tears!

Aunt Emma tried to comfort me, as she said that she had something to tell me. She told me that Uncle Willie molested her daughter and that if she had believed me, she could have prevented it from happening to her daughter. I was extremely surprised to hear it. The three of us held each other for a moment.

Then Aunt Emma said, "I heard that your mother had been molested too; that's why I've invited her over today, also." About a half-hour later, my mother came in crying. She sat down beside me, and while tears rushed down her face, she said, "I had to leave home because I tried to tell mom that Uncle Willie was molesting me, but she didn't believe me. Please believe me...I never thought that he would ever try to hurt you."

I angrily began to shout, "How could you have left me in this house!?" And she answered, "Your grandmother loved your Uncle Willie more than me, and she wouldn't listen to anything I had to say. No one believed me. I'm sorry; please forgive me. I wasn't healed enough to come and get you and raise you. Every time I looked at you, I was reminded of my past. I allowed your Uncle Willie to rob us both of a fruitful life and rob me of having a wonderful relationship with you."

I said to her, "I'm sorry that I was so angry and that I allowed so much time to go by without calling or coming to visit you. I allowed Uncle Willie to rob me of a peaceful life, and I allowed him to rob me of having a wonderful relationship with you, too."

"No, it was my fault and I'm sorry!" said Aunt Emma, "I should have believed you. Instead, I was angry; I just didn't want to believe that he could do such a thing! I'm so sorry!"

Just then, after my mother, Aunt Emma, and I apologized to each other, my niece walked in and said, "I'm glad Uncle Willie is dead, because he was touching me and hurting me too." That's when my mother held my niece and apologized to her. Then we all apologized to her; we told her that we were sorry for allowing it to happen to her.

Then my mother, Aunt Emma, her daughter, my niece, and I fell on our knees and prayed to God. In tears, we prayed and told the Lord that we were going to devote our lives to helping others who are presently being abused or who have suffered abuse.

*"Let's help stop the abuse together!"* Women of divine destiny, remember that "in your season of greatness," God is your source; everything else is a resource!

*Bear ye one another's burdens, and so fulfill the law of Christ* (Gal. 6:2).

*Laughter is good medicine! Whenever you've been deeply hurt and your heart is so pierced that you feel a heavy burden, read or think of something that's funny, and you'll receive some immediate relief! Also, please don't ever forget to read the Scriptures because the Word of God will provide you with everlasting relief.*

⚜

# When I Say I'm Broke, I'm Broke

A little old lady answered a knock on the door one day, only to be confronted by a well-dressed young man carrying a vacuum cleaner.

"Good morning," said the young man. "If I could take a couple of minutes of your time, I would like to demonstrate the very latest in high-powered vacuum cleaners."

"Go away!" said the old lady. "I haven't got any money!" and she proceeded to close the door. Quick as a flash, the young man wedged his foot in the door and pushed it wide open. "Don't be too hasty!" he said, "Not until you have at least seen my demonstration."

And with that, he emptied a bucket of horse manure onto her hallway carpet. "If this vacuum cleaner does not remove all traces of this horse manure from your carpet, Madam, I will personally eat the remainder."

The old lady stepped back and said, "Well I hope you've got a good appetite, because they cut off my electricity this morning."

*It's an old question: Why*
*should I forgive those who hurt me?*
*The answer to the question is:*

༄

# Forgiveness Is Necessary and Healing

The Bible says that we must forgive others in order for us to be forgiven (Matt. 6:12).

Forgiving the people who hurt me was one of the most difficult things that I have ever done. At first, it was hard, because the trespassers didn't appear to be remorseful; they also kept hurting me, in the same manner, over and over again. I felt that I couldn't get past the "old" stuff, and yet people were still filling me up with "fresh" hurts, by doing the same old stuff to hurt me, over and over again.

For years I felt that "something" was holding me back from being the person God created me to be. That "thing" that was holding me back was "unforgiveness."

I rationalized for years, saying to God, "They don't deserve forgiveness; what they did to me was too bad, and if they cared anything about you, God, or me, they wouldn't keep doing the same crazy stuff over and over. Obviously, they think that you're a joke, and never, ever, cared anything about me. Why should I forgive them?"

The truth is that I felt that they didn't deserve forgiveness. I sort of wanted God to tell me that my hurts were special and that I didn't have to forgive the people who hurt me.

My heart was filled with hate, resentment, revenge, anger, and bitterness. I had arthritis and severe stomach problems. I was constantly throwing up, and I kept experiencing severe sinus problems and colds. My resistance was always low; therefore, I couldn't really fight off colds or sinus infections.

However, the truth is this: When we don't forgive, we keep ourselves in darkness and the beauty of God's light is not over us. Unforgiveness blocks our blessings and keeps us from hearing and receiving from God.

When we don't forgive, we only hurt our relationship with God, and the enemy (satan) becomes stronger while our relationship with God becomes weaker.

One day, I fell down on my knees and told the Lord that I would do anything for Him, even forgive the people who hurt me so terribly. Although I thought that I was doing God a favor, the act of forgiveness healed my body and my spirit.

I didn't have any more headaches. I slept "good" at night. My days were filled with laughter, joy, and peace. I began to have a more victorious life. I thought about all those years that I wasted. I couldn't recoup those years, but I have vowed that I would never lose another minute to "unforgiveness." Anger and unforgiveness robbed me of a fruitful, prosperous life; but I won't allow it to rob me anymore!

Now I see why God so desperately wants us to forgive others. He wants us to live a whole, happy, fulfilling life. I thought that God wanted me to forgive…to help others, but God also wanted me to forgive because it released me; when I finally forgave others, I was set free! Forgiveness set me free!

All that time, God was trying to set me free, and I didn't know it. I just couldn't comprehend the fact that *I* was the one who was bound and burdened.

Forgiveness can set you free, too! Forgive those who have hurt you; then, begin walking in your divine destiny!

*Have you ever thought about giving up?*
*This story will help you hold on…*
*just a little while longer.*

ԑ੭

# Two Little Mice

There were once two mice; they fell into a bucket of crème.

The first mouse quickly gave up and drowned.

The second mouse wouldn't quit; he struggled so hard that he eventually turned that crème into butter.

Which mouse are you?

(The original source of this story is the movie *Catch Me If You Can*.)

*Are you your sister's keeper?*

৪৯

# My Sister's Keeper

My sister and I have always been extremely close; we grew closer with each passing day. She's a year older than I am, but people always said that we looked like twins. We've always shared everything and never kept anything from one another. She was more than a sister; she was my best friend, so quite naturally when she asked me if she could come and live with me, I said, "Yes, and you can move in immediately!"

We had so much fun together. We went shopping and played tennis and bowled together the way we used to when we were little girls; we've always loved tennis and bowling. Our lives seemed identical, except for one part; I was married, and my sister had never been married.

When we were children, we always talked about having a double wedding, living as neighbors, and having children who were as close to each other as we were.

I loved them both, my husband and my sister; that's why it was so hard for me to see them arguing all the time. They would fuss about any little thing. I couldn't stand to be in the same room with them, because whenever they saw each other, they would explode with anger. I hated the fact that they didn't get along together. They both meant a lot to me, and I didn't want to "take sides" or choose between them.

I tried everything to help them get along, and for a long while nothing helped until my husband, my sister, and I went on a family vacation. The three of us went on a cruise, and when we returned home, they weren't bickering the way they used to; they were getting along, and I was extremely happy. I guess we all needed to get away and unwind.

After we came back from our trip, I had to work overtime hours to catch up on some things. That's when it happened. A couple of days after we came back from our vacation I came home and found my sister in bed with my husband.

I slapped her before she knew what had hit her. I was screaming! I was enraged! My husband kept babbling something; I'm not sure what he was saying, and I didn't care. I began throwing anything that I could pick up—lamps, phones—at my husband. I'm sure that if I had a gun, I would have shot both of them. I am sure of that fact.

My sister ran out of the house barely clothed, but she was still alive, no thanks to me. I continued to throw things at my husband until he was finally able to run out of the house wearing only his underwear.

My husband moved in with his mother and later he left a message on our answering machine saying, "It didn't mean anything; this is all the result of a weak moment. Please forgive me. Please forgive me. I'd rather be dead than hurt you. I love you."

I haven't personally heard from my sister, but I heard from my husband's mother that my sister was pregnant and that it was my husband's baby.

I will never forgive my sister. I can't find it in my heart to forgive her. I can't begin to explain the pain that it caused me. I've been suffering through the stages of facing death (anger, denial, bargaining)—every stage but the "acceptance" stage.

I've been so betrayed. Sometimes, I wonder if there are other people who are experiencing the pain that I am, but I don't think that there is anyone else on earth who is hurting like me. I haven't had any rest or peace since I caught them together. I had no clue what was going on. I don't know when they started. I have so many unanswered questions, and no closure.

I hope that you never go through anything like this. However, if you happen to find yourself experiencing anything remotely close to this kind of sick predicament, I hope that you are stronger than me and that you'll be able to forgive.

### *Grandma Joy's P.S.*

When you can return love for betrayal or hate, you've found a purpose that will lead you to a divine destiny. Sin misdirects us and causes us to follow a false destiny, a destiny of destruction. If the victim can redirect her focus and begin praying and asking God to show her how to forgive, God will come inside of her heart and comfort her. He will deliver her from something that she feels is impossible to live through. God is waiting for her to come to Him. He wants to dry her tears and turn her sorrow into joy. He wants to lead her to a path of peace and righteousness.

### *Your thoughts*

What do you think that she should do about her marriage?

_____

_____

_____

_____

What would you do?

_____

_____

_____

_____

How should she handle the relationship with her sister? (You might need more room to answer this question. You can write more on another sheet of paper or just meditate on the answer in your mind, heart, and spirit.)

*Never despise the day of small beginnings.*

৪৯

# The Outhouse

We grew up poor. My mother and father had five boys and four girls. Our house in the country had three bedrooms. All the boys slept in one bedroom. All the girls slept in another bedroom, and our mother and father slept in the third bedroom.

Our mother washed, cooked, and cleaned for some folks in the city until she worked herself to death. Our father worked at a mill factory until he worked himself to death, and we had to live with our grandmother. Our roof leaked, and we set jars out to catch the water. It seemed to rain all the time!

Every Sunday morning, we would wake up to the smell of hot buttered biscuits dipped in molasses and the singing of *Amazing Grace* by grandma. Then, she would get us ready to go to Sunday school and church.

We could only go to school during "off seasons" when there was very little or no work to be done in the fields. When we were able to attend school, we learned reading, writing, and arithmetic.

However my brother June Bug learned even more. He learned to be ashamed of our grandma and our way of life. She didn't do it often, because she had to work in the fields, but once in a while grandma would walk for miles to get to our schoolhouse to see how we were doing. June Bug was very ashamed of her, because when she came to school, she was wearing clothes made from a feed sack. Her old boots would go "clickatty clack," because she had the blacksmith hammer horseshoes on the bottom of her boots. She said she got better wear out of them that way.

Grandma would send us to school with a greasy biscuit in a brown paper sack; June Bug wouldn't eat his food, because he was embarrassed. He didn't want anyone to know that he was poor. So he would give me his biscuit and he ate like a pig as soon as he got home from school.

At age 18, June Bug joined the Army. He said that he couldn't wait to leave our bamma, country hicktown, so that he could go out into the world and be somebody important and educated. "When I leave this bamma hicktown, I'm going to eat steak every day, not biscuits, molasses, and pig feet, and I'm not going to go to church every Sunday morning either," proclaimed June Bug.

On his first trip back home to visit us in our old dilapidated log cabin house, he brought a professor home with him. June Bug was taking a class at a university in the town where he was stationed.

Although June Bug had always said that we were just a bunch of backwoods, country hicks, this time was different. It wasn't until he found out that our grandma's ancestral roots and her antique items were extremely valuable to the uppity folks at the university that he began to claim us as "his folks."

He showed the professor all around our house, and they examined everything. They walked around with a notebook, camera, and a tape recorder while they examined our icebox and our foot tubs. They even examined the old slop jar that my granddaddy used when he was living. (A slop jar is used for spitting and urinating in.) It seemed strange to us that June Bug would be so proud of our way of living, the living he was ashamed of for so many years.

The rest of the family stood by and watched June Bug and the professor make fools of themselves. "Well, this is where I grew up. This is where I slept at night," said June Bug as he pointed to his old room and the old bed he used to sleep on.

June Bug showed the professor almost everything and the professor's eyes gleamed with excitement while June Bug held his head up high as he swelled with pride. "Here…here's a homemade biscuit dipped in molasses, hot out of our own oven. Please try one. Grandma sure put her foot in it this time!" said June Bug.

The two sat down and ate some of grandma's homemade biscuits, the same biscuits that June Bug was so ashamed of when he was going to school. "These are the best biscuits I've ever tasted," proclaimed the professor.

June Bug continued to brag about his humble beginnings, "Grandma and cousin Neckbone would shoot anything that moved, like squirrels, rabbits, and coons. Sometimes, they would kill a possum, bring it home, and cook it. They'd singe the hair off, scrap him, gut him, boil him, and bake him with spices and sweet potatoes. That was some good eating! Mmmm mmm…

…We'd eat possum, sweet potatoes, collard greens, and corn bread with our hands; it tasted better that way! It was even better if you had some crackling bread to go with it. Grandma made crackling by cooking fat back (from hogs) in a large wash pot. We also used old fat meat grease and lye to make soap. We used everything on the hog from the 'rooter to the tooter.' Those were the good ole' days. Look here…here's my grandma's Bible" (pointing to an old family Bible).

"You all must be some good Christian folks!" said the professor.

June Bug energetically replied, "Oh yes, we got up early every Sunday morning and went to Sunday school and church services. Throughout the week, grandma would pick cotton from sunup to sundown. In between picking cotton, making tubes of sausages, and washing chitterlings, grandma always had time to pray. Oh yes, we are some praying folks."

The professor picked up grandma's old smoothing iron and said, "Why this is truly a valuable antique item!"

June Bug swell with pride, and his eyes sparkled with greed. He said proudly, "Grandma used to use a smoothing iron to press our clothes; she'd heat the iron on coals and make starch with flour and water. We ain't rich folks; oh no, we just po' folks, but we had everything we needed. Yes, sir, this is the way we lived!"

June Bug and the professor were finishing their tour, but when it seemed as if they were about to leave, the professor looked in our backyard. He pointed and said, "What is that old, little building?"

June Bug had a puzzled look on his face as he answered the question, "That right there is our…outhouse."

"An outhouse, what is an outhouse? Can I take a look at it?" asked the professor.

"You don't want to go look in there," said June Bug.

"But, yes, I would like to go and look at that little house," said the professor.

June Bug held his head up high and strutted with the professor over to our outhouse. It's hard to describe the look on the professor's face when he opened the door of our outhouse. He looked like a cuckold who just found out his wife had been cheating on him for years and everyone knew it but him. The smell was unbearable, but that didn't stop the professor from taking pictures of our old, stinking outhouse.

"I have a treasure chest of information and materials to share with the other professors and students at the university. You must be extremely proud of your people and your way of life!" stated the professor as he and June Bug walked to the professor's fancy car.

"Yes, I am very proud of my people and our way of life," said June Bug.

We stood by and watched them leave, feeling sorry for them, knowing that they were the most ignorant people whom we'd ever met.

### *Grandma Joy's P.S.*

"Wherever you go, always remain humble and never forget to thank those who helped you along the way!"

*One of the things that Tyra Banks says to the contestants on her TV show is, "Being a supermodel involves more than just being physically beautiful." I think it is wonderful that she teaches the young ladies about the importance of **inner** beauty.*

৪৯

# Extreme Makeover

I'm sure that you've seen them…women who were physically attractive but their nasty attitude and personality made them appear ugly. You've probably also seen women who were physically unattractive but had beautiful personalities, so beautiful that they were absolutely gorgeous.

The truth is that you can get an extreme makeover from the best plastic surgeon in the world and still be ugly after the surgery, because true beauty is more than skin deep. America needs to start looking at beauty a different way. The old saying still holds true: Beauty is in the eye of the beholder.

When I was a teenager in high school, I didn't like being skinny, and I didn't like the way my mouth was shaped so I used to cover my mouth with my hands, especially when I talked. I had a large mouth with full lips and at night before I went to bed, I taped my mouth up. One day, a boy in my class asked me why I always covered my mouth, and he said, "You have a beautiful smile!" I will never forget him or how he made me feel.

After he told me that, I stopped covering my mouth, and I've been proud of my smile ever since. Now, I let the world see my big, beautiful smile everyday! If I had a dollar for everyone who told me that I had a beautiful smile, I'd surely be rich.

It was good that my high school classmate was able to influence me and change my attitude toward my appearance, but it was bad that I had such low self-esteem that I had to wait for a boy to validate me.

There are so many Christian women who can share their experiences with other women (oftentimes right in their own family or church) to inspire them and help them feel beautiful.

One of these women is Helen. Helen can teach us something about beauty even though she was born deaf and is slowly going blind. She has artificial arms and legs, because she lost her limbs due to a severe case of bacterial meningitis. Moreover, one side of her face was disfigured, so she avoided looking in mirrors. Unfortunately, though, people didn't let her forget what she looked like.

Her whole life people teased her, telling her how hideous and ugly she was. When she was a child, other children would call her "the creature from Star Trek." When she walked down the street, people would stare and point at her. All her life, she just wanted to look "normal."

For years, she was angry with God and with her parents because she believed that her impairments and sufferings were due to God punishing her parents for their sins. She was so angry, she couldn't get along with family members and had no friends. People didn't want to have anything to do with her, because she was so bitter and angry. She always wondered what it felt like to be pretty. However, she lived most of her life in a state of anomie and feeling suicidal.

For years, she suffered from extreme depression; she had been in and out of mental hospitals, and had been misdiagnosed several times. It seemed that no one could help her. In a desperate attempt at normalcy, Helen thought that if she could get an extreme makeover, she could live a better life and be happy. She did everything that she could to get enough money so that she could have surgery on her face and eyes.

When people tried to share the gospel of Jesus Christ with Helen, she would get angry and would often curse them out. She rejected anything that was related to Jesus.

She was 34 years old when her parents died, and she became an even angrier person after their death. When they were living, they begged her to seek God's face and turn her life over to God. One day, she fell on her knees and cried out to God, asking Him, "Why?" She stayed on her knees, because she was determined to get an answer from God, and God surely spoke to her that day. He told her that He created her for a reason.

After hearing His voice, she finally began reading her Bible, and she fell on her knees again and asked the Lord to come into her life and save her. She said, "Jesus, I believe that you are the Son of God. I don't want to look like a side-show freak or a monster anymore. I feel like I'm on the outside of life watching everyone else live it. All my life, I've heard that you have the power to deliver anyone from any problem or from any pain. Please come and help me. I want to begin serving you, and I want to know your love. I don't care if I'm not beautiful; I just want to look normal. Thank you, Amen."

She began to read God's Word, and God immediately changed her attitude and her life. The more of God's Word that she read the sweeter and more loving she became. She became so loving that she made friends for the first time in her life, and they invited her to their church which "just happened" to have a sign language interpreter. God was truly blessing her.

Helen thanked God for the new peace in her life, and she began to grow strong in the Lord. One day Helen made a vow to God. She told him that if He would send her a husband, she would devote her life to helping people learn of God's beauty.

Much to Helen's surprise and joy, God sent her a husband. She met Richard, who was also deaf and going blind, in church. Of all places, she met him in church. What are the odds of something like this happening naturally? It's a one in a million chance; therefore, we can credit the supernatural Spirit of God for this miracle, because it was surely God at work in Helen's life!

Helen and Richard volunteered their time teaching children with special needs how to use their abilities. Before Helen came into his life, Richard was lonely, and he had also asked the Lord to send him a mate. Before they met, Helen had never dated anyone. Men used to look at her as though she was hideous. When Richard met Helen, he fell in love with her inner beauty, wit, and charm.

Helen and Richard fell in love and got married; Helen was a beautiful bride. When other women who thought they had "supermodel" beauty saw Helen walk down the aisle of the church to get married, they were jealous and wanted to know Helen's secret. Helen, of course, didn't mind sharing that fact that God blessed her with a husband.

Although Helen and Richard were both slowly going blind, they continued to serve God. A year after they got married, they had a beautiful baby boy with no impairments or deformities.

Now, Helen uses her disfigured face and body to attract the attention of people who want to learn more about Jesus and how He can make anyone beautiful and happy. Helen and Richard began teaching people through seminars, and they traveled around the world teaching people about the beauty and love that God gives.

Helen received an extreme "spiritual" makeover from Jesus, and it didn't cost her a dime.

If Jesus can do it for her, He can do it for you! It's time to allow Jesus to give you an extreme makeover; envision yourself having an initial consultation with the Lord. What if He tells you that you can become beautiful without cosmetic surgery? What if He tells you that He can make you beautiful without spending a dime? That's exactly what Jesus is waiting to tell you.

*Fall down on your knees and allow God to shape and model you. God wants to adorn you with glory. He wants to give you the garment of praise for the spirit of heaviness, beauty for your ashes, and the oil of glory for your mourning. He wants to recreate you perfectly and beautifully!*

*We need the love and support of each other. No one can do it alone! Of the following two stories, "It Takes a Village" is a folktale and "More Than Conquerors" is based on Scripture—both have important messages for your whole community. The stories "A Mother's Love" and "Missing Out" are contemporary stories with important messages for your entire family. Please share and enjoy these stories with your family and with members of your community.*

৵৹

# It Takes a Village

In a small village long ago, all was well. Everything ran smoothly, because everyone worked together. The elders would teach the children, and the children would listen.

One day, though, the young adults came together and held a meeting for young people only. "The elderly people are too slow. They talk funny, and they shouldn't be around our children," announced a young person. "Yes, those old ways are not good for our children. We need to get rid of all the old folks so that we can get rid of all the old ways and create a modern village. Change is what we need," said another young person. It was agreed at the meeting that the elderly people were not needed and that they would be sent away to an island to live together.

All the elderly were gathered together in a boat and sent away. "We'll send you everything that you need to take good care of youselves," promised the young people, as they waved goodbye.

With all the elderly people gone, the young adults thought that they would have a perfect, modern village. Things changed, but not for the better. Without the elderly people, the young people wasted food and money. The young people did not know how to plant the crops, and they did not know how to care for the sick. Without the elderly people, the children were unhappy and disobedient. The babies would cry for the elderly, and the children did not go to school.

The young people had another meeting and said, "Oh, we need the elderly people. We cannot do it all alone. Let's get our elderly and bring them back home." The youth hurried to get the elderly and brought them back.

With the return of the elderly, all was well in the village again. The young people confessed, "It takes a village to have a good harvest and keep things running smoothly. It takes a village to raise a child."

# More Than Conquerors

God's people were being threatened by an army that the enemy had formed. Everyone had *heard* that the enemy's army was big and strong and that they had powerful weapons. Because many people believed that the enemy's army was bigger and stronger, they feared the enemy and allowed the enemy to overtake their land and rob them of peace, hope, and joy. The enemy had a false reputation of being fierce giants who were undefeated. They used these false legends about their false powers to scare people into joining their army.

While the enemy was spreading rumors and tales about their power, God raised up a true army of soldiers in the name of Jesus. There weren't many of these Christian soldiers, but they were courageous. They prayed without ceasing, as well as read God's Word and worshiped Him through song and praise. After days of prayer and praise, the Lord revealed to the leader of His army in a dream that they were going to be more than conquerors and that they would have the victory over the enemy.

The army of soldiers for Jesus did not doubt God. When they were confronted by the enemy's army, they stood faithful and confident.

When the enemy's army saw God's army, they said among themselves, "They have a very small army, but they appear to be very sure of something. They would not be this confident unless they have something that we can't see. They have secret weapons and secret powers. They have something that we don't have, and we can't take a chance. We better turn back and go home or they will defeat us with their unseen powers."

Fearing and trembling, the enemy's army ran away as fast as they could and told everyone in the land that there is a "giant" army of Christian soldiers who are fierce and strong with unseen powers. Everyone *heard* about the strength of God's army. Through obedience and faith, God's army took back the land that belonged to the saints of God, renewing their peace, hope, joy, and love. As time passed, people heard about God's army and joined His army. Today, God's army is still a peaceful, loving army. The people in His army continue to grow big and strong. They are undefeated and victorious. They have power to resist sin and the power to live happier, more prosperous lives. The members of the mighty Army of God will forever be more than conquerors. Through Christ they will overcome the enemies of this world and live forever with God in Heaven.

Whose army will you join?

*Everyone needs to know the beauty of a mother's love!*

# A Mother's Love

There was once a mother who had a son. When he was young, he wanted expensive toys that he saw on television. His mother couldn't afford them. She said, "We'll read our Bible, because everything we need, we can get from the Word of God." He got angry and had a temper tantrum.

When he grew older and went to middle school, he saw other kids with expensive clothes. He asked his mother to buy him brand-name clothes, but she couldn't afford them. She said, "Read your Bible, son, and you will find out that everything you need is in the Scriptures, in the Word of God."

When he grew older and became a teenager, he saw some of his high school friends with new cars. He asked his mother to buy him an expensive new car, but she couldn't afford it. She said, "Please, son, read your Bible; study the Scriptures, because you will find everything you need, even things you want, in the Word of God." He got angry.

He got angry with her and began to stay out all night with his friends. And because his mother was so worried about him, she got sick and had to go to the hospital. Her son never knew about all the sacrifices that she had been making for many years to take care of him.

For years, she couldn't afford to buy her blood pressure pills and her heart medicine. For years, she wore raggedy shoes that hurt her feet. She had to buy lots of vegetables to cook and serve for meals because she couldn't always afford to buy meat. Her son would complain about having to always eat vegetables.

Yet the biggest surprise came when her son found out that his mother was in the hospital on Mother's Day. He rushed to see her as soon as he heard the news. When he arrived, he hugged and kissed her and said, "Mother, I have that Bible that you always tried to get me to read. We'll read it together." He opened the Bible and flipped through it. As he searched through the Bible for a comforting Scripture to read to her, he saw money falling out from between the pages.

Then he saw a little note in his mother's handwriting: "To my son, On your graduation day, this is the down payment on your new car. Love, Mom."

For years, she had been making sacrifices in order to save enough money for a down payment on a new car as a gift for him when he graduated from high school.

Finally he realized that throughout his entire life, he already had the most valuable gift of all—the gift of a mother's love.

"Happy Mother's Day"

# Missing Out

There once lived a young girl named Jennifer. Jennifer lived with her father who was a carpenter and a gardener. He was a single parent and he worked very hard to take care of her.

Every family is different. Some families have two people, some three or more. Some families have foster children. Some families have a stepmother, or a stepfather, and stepchildren. Some families have adopted children, and some families have a grandmother or grandfather (an extended family) as part of the household.

In order to keep things running smoothly in a family, everyone has to do their share of work. Jennifer had to do her share of the work in her family. She had to wash the dishes, sweep the floors, help her father in the garden, and do homework every day before she could go outside to play.

Every day the kids would ride by Jennifer's house on bicycles and skates and tease her by saying, "Jennifer's missing out! Jennifer's missing out! That Jennifer is sure missing out!"

One day Jennifer asked her father, "Daddy, why do we have to work so hard? Why? No one else works as hard as we do." Her father said, "Jennifer, we work hard now, but we will get our reward later. If you plant a good seed, you'll receive a good crop. Jennifer, why don't we go for a ride? Let's do something different. You deserve a break!"

Jennifer and her father went for a ride in their old, broken-down car. While they were riding, they saw an elderly homeless man on a street corner. Jennifer's father stopped the car to give the man food and money. Jennifer laughed and said, "Look at that old bum. He's sure missing out!"

Her father, who loved her, was shocked and disappointed. He said, "Jennifer, I'm surprised at you. I've taught you better. Why would you say such things?"

"Daddy, I know it's wrong to tease. I just did it because the other kids do it. I don't mean any harm, but he is an old bum, and he sure is missing out," said Jennifer.

Jennifer's father said, "Jennifer, I'll give you some advice, and I want you to take this with you wherever you go. You can learn something from anyone. You can learn from an old person, from a young, even from a homeless person. I want you to remember three things. *One*...learn to be thankful and appreciative for your family; you have a parent who loves you. *Two*...realize that to live comfortably, you must work hard. *Three*...learn never to miss out on a good opportunity to bless someone, to help someone. Never miss out! Never miss out!"

Jennifer never forgot her father's words. She continued to work hard at home and at school. *She grew up and became a doctor.* She got married and had two beautiful children, Zachery and Mary. She and her family lived in a beautiful home and they were very happy. Jennifer was happy to live in a two-parent home, and she and her husband raised their children like they were raised.

One day, Jennifer and her husband decided that they would take their children to see their grandfather. While driving in their brand new car, they saw a young, homeless person on a street corner. Jennifer said, "Good husband, good husband, let's stop and help." Jennifer's husband said, "Good wife, good wife, yes, let's stop and help." They agreed to stop and help the homeless person on the corner. Their children were happy that their parents were loving people. Jennifer and her husband gave the man food, money, and purchased him new clothes.

The homeless man said, "Thank you for all you've done for me. You've given me more than what money can buy. You've encouraged my heart. I really appreciate all you've done for me, but I have one question. Jennifer, (although Jennifer never told him her name, he called her by her name) why would you stop and help me after I laughed and teased you as a child? I was a bully and everyone knows that bullies are just jealous. I knew you were going to succeed in life. You worked hard, and you had a parent who loved you. Now, you're a doctor, and you have a beautiful family. Why would you stop and help me after I laughed and teased you as a child?"

Jennifer said, "Because I do not want, I do not want, I do not want to *miss out!*"

*The following are helpful hints for…*

ℬ

# America's Next Top Mom

↬ Have dinner with your children. Taking time out of your busy schedule to have dinner with your children is healthy and important. This gives you an opportunity to bond with your children and show them that you love them.

↬ Pray with your children (make it a tradition in your home), and teach them that they are never too young to pray.

↬ Set aside one night a week for family discussions and family planning. Together your family can discuss subjects like smoking, drinking, and violence. Your family can also discuss your plans for the following week, such as meals and fun activities for the whole family. Talking to your children can help them discover new ways to handle their problems. It can also become a special time to share memories, laughter, and love. If you have trouble discussing matters with your children, just start by telling jokes and laughing together. Telling them about your most embarrassing moment is a great icebreaker. Your support and love is crucial to your children's success. Ask them while riding in your car, "What do you want to become when you grow up?" Encourage them; give them confidence! You can also play the game "Punch Bug" while riding in your car. Always enjoy the special time you spend with your children. You have more to offer them than you may realize.

ᴥ Remember to always reward your children for their successes at home as well as for their academic work in school. Try to find ways to give them unusual rewards such as rewarding them for being courteous to their siblings. You can even reward your children for being patient and playing fair. Of course, you'll want to also reward them for doing their chores around the house and for doing their homework. *It is very important to inform your children that they will not always be perfect, but (at the same time) you should always encourage them to be the best person that they can be.* Some non-monetary rewards can be a sleepover party or an ice cream party.

ᴥ You can't always physically be with your children, but there are some special things that you, as America's Next Top Mom, can do to comfort your children while they experience nervousness during a hospital visit, first day school, during tests, or even on their graduation day. Fill your children's school notebook with fun pictures of themselves spending time with family and friends. They can bring these special pictures with them to their hospital room and these special photos will remind them of the love and support that their family gives them. Also, don't forget about having Scriptures in their notebooks and in picture frames beside their hospital beds. Scriptures will always comfort your children, and if they learn early to rely on God's Word, they'll be more prone to rely on His Word later when they are adults!

ॐ

# The Four Wives

There was a rich merchant who had four wives. He loved the fourth wife the most and adorned her with rich robes and treated her to delicacies. He took great care of her and gave her nothing but the best.

He also loved the third wife very much. He was very proud of her and always wanted to show her off to his friends. However, the merchant was always in great fear that she might run away with some other man.

He loved his second wife too. She was a very considerate person, always patient and in fact was the merchant's confidante. Whenever the merchant faced problems, he always turned to his second wife and she would help him and tide him through difficult times.

Now, the merchant's first wife was a very loyal partner and had made great contributions in maintaining his wealth and business as well as taking care of the household. However, the merchant did not love the first wife and although she loved him deeply, he hardly took notice of her.

One day, the merchant fell ill. Before long, he realized he was going to die. He thought of his luxurious life and told himself, "Now I have four wives with me. But when I die, I'll be alone. How lonely I'll be!"

Thus, he asked his fourth wife, "I loved you most, endowed you with the finest clothing and showered great care over you. Now that I'm dying, will you follow me and keep me company?" "No way!" replied the fourth wife and she walked away without another word.

The answer cut like a sharp knife right into the merchant's heart. The sad merchant then asked his third wife, "I have loved you so much for all my life. Now that I'm dying, will you follow me and keep me company?" "No!" replied the third wife. "Life is so good over here! I'm going to remarry when you die!" The merchant's heart sank and turned cold.

He then asked his second wife, "I always turned to you for help and you've always helped me. Now I need your help again. When I die, will you follow me and keep me company?" "I'm sorry, I can't help you this time!" replied the second wife. "At the very most, I can only send you to your grave." The answer came like a bolt of thunder and the merchant was devastated.

Then a voice called out: "I'll leave with you. I'll follow you no matter where you go." The merchant looked up and there was his first wife. She was so skinny, almost like she suffered from malnutrition. Greatly grieved, the merchant said, "I should have taken much better care of you while I could have!"

Actually, we all have four "wives" in our lives:

1. The fourth wife is our body. No matter how much time and effort we lavish in making it look good, it'll leave us when we die.

2. Our third wife is our possessions, status, and wealth. When we die, they all go to others.

3. The second wife is our family and friends. No matter how close they are to us when we are alive, the longest they can stay by us is up unto the grave.

4. The first wife is, in fact, our soul which is often neglected in our pursuit of material wealth and sensual pleasure.

*Guess what? Our soul is actually the only thing that follows us wherever we go. Perhaps it is a good idea to cultivate and strengthen the inner you now, rather than to wait until we are on our deathbed to lament.*

ℰ∂

# Desperate Housewives

My best friend was also my neighbor. We were both desperate housewives addicted to prescription drugs and bingo. Before I moved to the neighborhood, I considered myself to be a good wife and mother. Before I moved to the neighborhood, I didn't abuse drugs or gamble.

When I moved into the neighborhood, my neighbor offered to take my children to school every day with her children; I was extremely grateful. Every day, after dropping the kids off at school, she and I would spend time talking and watching soap operas together. While her husband was at work, she would load up on household drugs. In the beginning, I would just watch her abuse over-the-counter drugs like cough and cold medicine, but she slowly progressed to taking stronger drugs. She frequently went to her doctor to get certain prescribed drugs, and she spent almost all her money at the pharmacy.

Then one day, she asked me to do a favor for her. She asked if I would go to my family doctor complaining of severe pain in my body, severe anxiety, headaches, and sleeplessness. She wanted me to try to sway the doctor into giving me her "drugs of choice" which were Percocet, OxyContin, and Valium.

In order to make it through a day, my neighbor had to take a drug to pick her up in the morning and a drug to bring her back down at night before bedtime. The stimulant drug she chose was Ritalin. It was prescribed for her son even though he wasn't hyperactive. She accused him of having the disorder to get a doctor to write a prescription…just so she could use the drug.

In the beginning, I tried to talk her out of her addiction, but I soon found that there was nothing that I could say or do to change things. I felt that she might be a danger to herself and the children, so I offered to drive the children to school every morning.

For a long time, I was the sober, sensible one between the two of us, but that didn't last long. One night, my husband and I got into a big fight, and he left me. He packed his bags and moved out. I became very depressed and began taking some of the drugs that my neighbor had been taking for years.

It wasn't long before I was going to different doctors to get drugs for both my neighbor and myself. I soon became an expert; I learned what symptoms would get me certain types of drugs. I learned exactly what to tell the doctors and what not to say to them. If a doctor didn't give me exactly what I wanted, I would say, "I need a second opinion; could you refer me to another doctor?" Even if that doctor gave me the drug I wanted, I would still (oftentimes) pretend that I needed a second opinion. When all the second opinions ran out in our area, my neighbor and I went out of town to new doctors and would start the process all over again.

Soon, neither of us was fit to drive the children to school, so they missed lots of days. They were also missing doctor appointments, so we had trouble getting some of the drugs that we were taking, drugs like Ritalin.

In order to get more drugs, my neighbor would baby-sit children of friends (especially children who were hyperactive) so that she could raid their medicine cabinets. Finding the right kind of drug was hard to do this way, so we had to find other ways.

Therefore, in order to help supply our habits, I soon took my son to the doctor in an effort to get Ritalin for him so that my neighbor and I could get more of it for ourselves. In order to assure that he would be diagnosed correctly, we had him rehearse (fake) his hyperactivity over and over again in front of us. We made him practice until he got it right. He didn't just practice his hyperactivity in front of the doctor, but he had to also pretend to be hyper in front of his teacher at school (during the whole school day).

Years ago, this would have been unthinkable for me; I would never have done such a thing. But things had changed, because...now...I was an official addict. I became addicted to prescription drugs, and *the fact is that an untreated addict will do anything.*

The only way that an untreated addict can get help is...if/when the addict (first) admits that he/she is addicted to drugs. That wasn't something that my neighbor and I intended to do.

My son was referred to a behavioral specialist, and my husband took him to the appointment. By this time, I had sold our car and almost all the furniture in our house to get money to support my drug habit. During the session, my son disclosed the fact that he was coached to perform his illness.

My addiction was discovered, and my children were taken from me and placed in foster care. I was forced to face my addiction. I had to attend rehabilitation and go to family counseling. I thought that it was the end of the world for me. At least my husband's family was able to get custody of our children.

My neighbor never got caught; however, she eventually felt the need to take stronger drugs. Each day, she searched for a more intense high. She learned how to make methamphetamine from allergy/sinus products. She made a purified form of methamphetamine called crystal "ice," until it became easier to buy crack off the street than to make methamphetamine.

She soon became a crack addict. But she kept searching for a bigger and better high, so she tried heroin and eventually became a heroin addict. In order to get money to fund her heroin addiction, she smuggled heroin and money through airport security.

She never got caught, but it wasn't long after she became addicted to heroin that she died of a heroin overdose. Before she died, she married addiction. After her death, I married truth; I didn't know how lost I was until my children were taken away from me and until my neighbor died. My neighbor's death was sobering to me. I vowed never to abuse drugs again.

I am no longer a desperate housewife. My husband and I eventually got a divorce, and I went back to college and became a counselor. Now I help other desperate housewives who have become prescription drug addicts.

Sincerely,
*A Woman of Divine Destiny*

# SECTION II

## Great Women of the Bible and Their Divine Purpose

*The following Bible stories are about women who were pioneers of the gospel. If these great women of God could speak to you today, what would they say? Well, these women **are** speaking. They're speaking through the Scriptures and through the hearts and minds of every Christian woman wise enough to listen.*

*The following story (about the woman with the issue of blood) was written uniquely, because the woman's experience was so unique. As you read, ask yourself, "What would I do if I were in a similar situation? Would I have the faith that she had?"*

Ɠ

# Who Touched Me?

I'm a woman just like you, except my journey started many years ago. The people in my town were always talking about me and judging me, especially the men, but they had no clue about my plight; men were especially ignorant about that special day when I was healed by our Lord and Savior.

I must tell you about that particular day. It was a day when no one cared to gossip about me. That day, they were busy and excited about a new event, a new matter at hand. Jesus was in town, walking around healing people!

Because of my condition, men labeled me "unclean" (according to Lev. 15:25-31). I suffered with an issue of blood for 12 years. And since I was continuously "unclean" for so many years, I could not go to the temple and worship. I could not touch anyone, or they would be unclean for the rest of the day. If I sat in a chair, it was unclean for the rest of the day, etc. Therefore, I was basically cut off from normal fellowship with others and with God.

There were so many people all around me pushing and pulling that the crowd pushed me, and I fell down on my knees. But I could still see Him; there was a glow around Him. And with each step He took, the earth shook, rumbled, because His steps were ordered. I saw Him, that divine man of God, coming my way, so I waited while being trampled on. I waited while people kicked me in my face and stepped on my hands, but I didn't care how much pain I had to endure; I was determined to get just one touch.

The men in town were always saying that if something clean touches something unclean, then the thing that was clean is defiled. But this was not so with Jesus. With every miracle, this man of God, Jesus, cleanses the person He touches without contaminating Himself! This man of God is amazing!

*(Jesus "transfers" cleanliness and power; this is parallel to the spiritual healing that Jesus brings when He cleanses us of our sin today.)*

I thought to myself, "For if I may touch just the hem of His garment, I shall be made whole!"

Before this day men were cruel to me, and I suffered much at the hands of doctors. I had been to doctor after doctor, and I spent all I had (all my money) and did not get better; instead, I grew worse. Doctors used me as a guinea pig. They were experimenting with my body, but after all my money was gone, they didn't experiment any more. I was penniless, and doctors had no compassion; they would say, "Well, this is just another one of those 'women's problems,' and some women have problems. Just deal with it" (would be the words translated for modern day understanding).

But this man of God was different. He could count the very hairs on my head. I believe that He knew me before I was even born.

I continued to crawl around on the ground. My knees were all blistered and sore. I was extremely weak and tired. I could barely hold my head up. As people walked around me, they kicked dirt in my face. There was so much dust on the ground, I could barely see Him, but I could still sense that He was close by. Because I couldn't see His face anymore, I had to feel my way though the crowd.

Then, it happened! It was like a bolt of lightning! I'd finally touched His clothes, and I was made whole!

Jesus asked, "Who touched my clothes?" I came to him fearing and trembling and told Him all the truth. He replied, "Daughter, thy faith hath made thee whole; go in peace, and be whole of thy plague." I knew after meeting Him that I had a divine purpose in life, a purpose greater than any earthly man could envision. I knew that one day people would hear my story, and many would surrender their lives to Christ. (See Mark 5:25-34.)

Although there were countless people pulling and grabbing Jesus, He felt a special touch from the woman with the issue of blood. Jesus offers *"peace,"* to the women today and He gives His special peace to every woman He heals.

It doesn't matter how great your sins are. It is time for all women to accept the peace that Jesus offers us. Repent and forget all your sins, because they have all been forgiven. Now, daughter, Jesus wants you to go...in peace and be whole of your plague!

*Both Ruth and Esther were obedient women of God. They were both divinely lead by God and they reached a wonderful unexpected end! God rewarded their faithfulness and unselfishness. During a time of famine and danger, they were able (by God's grace) to marry prestigious, high-ranking men and help themselves and their families.*

*Like Joseph, everything that Ruth and Esther encountered worked together for their "good" and caused them to become great women of God—walking in their divine purpose. Things happened to them that they never dreamed would happen, and things are going to happen to you that you never dreamed could happen!*

*You may already be familiar with the scenario of the story. If so, you'll fall in love with its beauty all over again. If you're not already familiar with the Book of Ruth, please read the Book of Ruth from the Bible first; then, come back to this book, and I will continue sharing ideas with you. The Book of Ruth is a beautiful expression of God's love and faithfulness.*

కా

# Ruth

During this time in the Book of Ruth, sin was rampant, spreading widely. Every man lived according to his own personal perception of the laws. And, of course, they interpreted the law to only suit themselves. In those days, it was rare to meet anyone who had great faith.

Also, there was a famine in the land. Rainfall in Palestine was never very plentiful, and quite frequently it was insufficient to provide adequately for raising basic crops. Ruth and Orpah were daughters-in-law of Naomi; the three of them lived in Moab alone, because Naomi's husband and her two sons died (the husbands of Ruth and Orpah). Naomi became bitter and changed her name to Mara (which means "bitter").

Naomi decided to go back to her native land, Bethlehem in Judah. She did not expect her daughter-in-law, Ruth, to be so faithful and leave her native land, Moab, to go with her to Judah. This was considered an unusual act of faithfulness on Ruth's part, because Ruth could have stayed in Moab and remarried. It was also a tribute to the Godly character of Naomi that her daughter-in-law was prepared to leave her own land to go with Naomi to Judah. Orpah did not follow them. Although the character of Orpah is in direct contrast with that of Ruth's, no word of reproach is intended for Orpah. Orpah loved Naomi, but she didn't love her God (the God of Israel) enough to leave her native land. Analogously, many of us have the love of Christ, but we fall short when it comes to obeying His will.

While Ruth had a vision to be comforted by her own faithfulness, Orpah felt that it was too risky to leave all that she knew and start over in a foreign land. However, Ruth faithfully announced to her mother-in-law, *"Whither thou goest, I will go; and where thou lodgest, I will lodge; thy people shall be my people, and thy God my God: Where thou diest, will I die, and there will I be buried: the Lord do so to me, and more also, if ought but death part thee and me"* (Ruth 1:16-17). Ruth renounced all that she could be expected to hold dear in Moab (people she had known all her life, possibility of marrying a Moabite man, her culture, and understanding of the land), and she voluntarily chose to go to Judah and there begin an entirely "new life" with her mother-in-law. Ruth was faithful and became a covenant woman of God! In Moab, Ruth would have been expected to worship Chemosh (Num. 21:29). However, in Judah, she would worship the God of Israel. Ruth was willing to entrust herself to the God of Israel whom they (now) worshiped. When Naomi returned to Bethlehem with her daughter-in-law, it was harvest season! They came "at the right time and season!"

Oh great woman of God, like Naomi and Ruth, this is your season! It is harvest time! Don't be afraid to leave everything behind that died in a desert land and to begin worshiping the true God, the God of Israel, where there is life! Your faith in God will cause you to move into your divine destiny! Remember, your present situation cannot dictate where you're going in God. Faith is believing in things "as though they were." *Faith is the substance of things hoped for, the evidence of things not seen* (Heb. 11:1).

With faith, I can say, "What I see is temporal, but what I don't see is eternal!" Naomi had a kinsman (relative) named Boaz. Although Naomi and Ruth were poor, God gave them favor and Ruth married

Boaz. Their marriage restored all the land and wealth that Naomi's family lost. God will give you favor with men!

Boaz inquired, "Who is that beautiful maiden?" He was told by his servant that Ruth was nobody special, just a second-class field hand. (Normally, a person of Ruth's poor classification wouldn't be able to glean the fields until after all the reapers finished; then, the poor people could gather all that was left behind in the fields.) Obviously, Boaz's servant could not see the "investment" that God had placed into His faithful Christian, Ruth.

She may have been a second-class citizen in the eyes of men, but it was through God's divine providence that Boaz would see Ruth working in the fields, fall in love with her, and marry her. It was God's divine destiny that Ruth had remained a clean, "upright," faithful woman of God.

Oh great woman of God, continue to stay pure, clean, and upright, because it is your season to reap rewards from Almighty God! There are times when you won't be able to explain why you're "leaving a desert land" (spiritually dry place of famine) to go to a new place, but you will know that you must go. And when you start your journey with worshiping God like you've never worshiped Him before, you'll know you are on the right path.

Oh great woman of God, if you see that all your friends and family members have become complacent because they are afraid to leave what they understand and are comfortable with, tell them that you have to move! Tell them that your God, the God of Israel, is calling you and that you have to obey God. Allow a mighty move of God in your life! And, if all your friends shake their heads and laugh, say to them, "Don't shake your heads at me because of the life I've suffered. Look at me through the mind of God! You will see that God will take care of me!" God never reveals himself as "I was." God is an "I am" God! God is a "now" God and a God of the future! We must have "present" faith to assure "future" manifestation.

Naomi and Ruth came to Bethlehem "at the beginning" when everything was right! This is *your* season for greatness. This year you might think that you just "stumbled" upon your blessings, but your blessings were set in your path on purpose. These blessings aren't haphazard blessings; your blessings from God are waiting for you. Just stay on the right path. God will order the laborers that came before you to "intentionally" save the harvest for you.

The story of Ruth supports the fact that: If God is for you, no man can be against you. No weapon formed against you shall prosper! (See Romans 8:31 and Isaiah 54:17). The enemy expects you to get depressed while you're in your dry season and to give up seeking God before you receive your blessings. Don't!

Boaz said to his servants, "Allow blessings to fall down in Ruth's path on purpose! Let her drink of the water provided for others. Allow no one to hurt Ruth or bother her! I will take care of her!" Right now, woman of God, (like Naomi's advice to Ruth) it is time to cleanse yourself because you are "going before the almighty King." Take off the old stuff and put on new garments. Then humble yourself at the feet of the almighty King. And stay there until you receive more instructions.

Oh great woman of God, give God the glory. A great work has already begun in your life, and God will finish what He started! After Boaz and Ruth were married, they were blessed with a son named Obed; his name means "worship." You, too, will spiritually birth a new life, even if your womb is dried up like Naomi's, because the seeds you are carrying aren't physical.

You may ask, "How can a woman carry seeds and birth something if her womb is dry?" It can and will be done for you, because God has a divine plan to deliver His divine words of salvation to all people. The words of God inside of you are spiritual seeds, and they will be planted and will grow! You, great woman of God, have been redeemed! You've already been delivered. Now it's time for you to walk in your divine destiny!

*You may already be very familiar with the scenario of
this story. If so, you'll fall in love with this story all over again.
If you're not already familiar with the Book of Esther,
please read the Book of Esther from the Bible first; then,
come back to this book, and I will continue sharing
ideas with you. The Book of Esther is a beautiful story!*

☙

# Esther

Mordecai was Esther's cousin. Mordecai raised Esther; he took her (his uncle's orphaned daughter) into his own home and raised her. He was like a father to Esther.

After Xerxes divorced queen Vashti, it was proposed that a new queen be chosen for him from among the most beautiful virgins in the land. Esther, a young Jewess, was among those brought to the palace. Xerxes loved Esther more than any other and chose her to be his queen. (Xerxes did not know that that Esther was a Jew.) Mordecai instructed Esther to keep her nationality a secret.

One day, Mordecai (who stood at the gate of the palace) discovered a plot against the king. Mordecai told Esther about the matter, and Esther warned the king. The criminals were executed. Later, Mordecai refused to bow before Haman, whom Xerxes had elevated to the second position in the kingdom. Mordecai wouldn't bow, because he was faithful and loyal to Jehovah, the true and living God. Consequently, Haman's wrath was aroused against Mordecai's nation.

As a result of Mordecai's refusal to bow to him, and because Haman promised the king all that he would confiscate from the Jews, Haman sought permission to destroy all Jews. Haman told the king that the Jews were defying his laws. The king gave Haman permission to destroy the Jews. Haman sent letters to the entire empire in the king's name, announcing the day of the Jews' destruction.

Haman asked the astrologers and magicians to cast the lot to determine which day of the year would bring destruction to Israel. The men of that day placed great confidence in astrology. But little did they realize that God had everything under control, and no weapon formed against His people could ever prosper! During the time before the date of destruction of the Jews, Esther and Mordecai remained faithful family members to each other. They sent messages back and forth to each other. Esther was a great woman of God; she sent a message back to Mordecai, saying, "We need to fast for three days. Fast ye for me! I and my maidens will, likewise, fast. And, if I perish, I perish!"

Glory to God; Esther's words are unforgettable. She said, "If I perish, I perish!" When you are going through trials and tribulation, don't worry about your own life, because if you take a bold stand for God, He will not allow you to perish. But be willing to do whatever it takes.

Mordecai obeyed Esther's request, and they fasted together. In the meantime, Esther invited the king and Haman to a banquet. At the banquet, the king offered to grant any request that Esther might have; she asked that they come to another banquet the next day. Even Haman was overjoyed at the special invitations, but he was still angry over Mordecai's refusal to bow before him.

On the third day of the fast, Esther obtained favor in the king's sight, remarkable evidence of the fact that the king's heart is in the hand of the Lord as the rivers of water: God "turneth it however he wishes!" Never underestimate the power of a woman in the kitchen, her faith in God, and her strong will to save her family! As time passed, Esther received "much" more favor in the king's sight, but the tables turned for Haman. Unable to sleep one night, the king had his official chronicles read to him, which told of Mordecai's unrewarded loyalty in exposing a plot against the king's life.

During Esther's second banquet, she asked the king for the preservation of her people from destruction and boldly accused Haman of being the adversary. The king went into the garden enraged at this discovery and returned to find Haman pleading with Esther for his life. Accusing him of attacking the queen, he ordered Haman to be hanged on the same gallows he had built for Mordecai. This was surely God's divine providence at work!

Earlier Haman was given a ring; later that same ring along with Haman's property and position was given to Mordecai (when the king remembered that Mordecai saved his life by informing him of the plot of the gatekeepers). Surely, divine providence was at hand. Because of Esther, who was faithful to Mordecai's instructions and her obedience to God, God spared the lives of all the Jews. And the special insignia ring was taken off Haman's finger, and it was given to Mordecai. Mordecai was appointed chief minister of the empire.

Esther said, "If I perish, I perish!" Nevertheless, it was God's divine providence that Esther live a long and prosperous life!

*Next, you will read several stories about Jesus
and His encounters with women. These
are not ordinary women. They are
women with a divine destiny!*

ஜ

# To Kiss His Feet

Jesus had an encounter with a woman who was labeled a prostitute. While Jesus was talking to men "with authority," this woman washed His feet with her tears and wiped them with the hairs on her head. She kissed his feet, and anointed them with ointment.

Luke 7:37-38 says:

*"And, behold, a woman in the city, which was a sinner, when she knew that Jesus sat at meat in the Pharisee's house, brought an alabaster box of ointment. And stood at his feet behind him weeping and began to wash His feet with tears, and did wipe them with the hairs of her head, and kissed his feet, and anointed them with the ointment."*

Please note that the Pharisees weren't considered "ordinary men." They considered themselves great men of God! They labeled themselves "the true worshipers of God." They believed that they were followers of "the letter law." While the Pharisees (thinking themselves "high-ranking") gathered to discuss important matters with Jesus, there was an intrusion of a sinner woman.

This intrusion was considered intolerable to the respectable Pharisee because of her evil reputation, because she was not an "invited guest," and also because she was a woman. Women did not have the same rights as men and especially these men who were considered of high rank.

Alabaster was a fine translucent stone, used mainly to make decorative pieces. The box of ointment was obviously very valuable and was possibly the proceeds from her sin (prostitution). She might have (usually) only used it (when prostituting) to make more money from it. Any other usage would be considered a waste. The men could not understand why she would "waste the ointment on Jesus."

However, the men would have accepted the idea of her using the ointment to provide them with physical pleasures. They would have accepted her into the room if she had come to give them sexual pleasures.

But, instead, she came to worship Jesus with all she had, and she used her long hair, her tears, and the expensive ointment to do so. The Pharisees wanted to "make sense" of everything around them. They would not have condemned her for doing what she normally did (acts of prostitution), and it was possible every man present had had "dealings" with her because they all knew her well.

This theory can be proven by the fact that she was in the house or in the vicinity of these men in the first place. While it is true that she wasn't invited into the room where Jesus was, she was "already within close quarters" with these men for a reason. She didn't come in off the street. Even today people want to enjoy life behind closed doors, and they do not want to make sacrifices in public. Jesus says that we must not be "of the world." People embrace the world, and flee away from God and anything divine or sacrificial!

In those days, guests at dinner did not sit at tables but reclined on couches with their heads toward the table. It would have been easy for this woman to kneel at the end of the couch on which Jesus lay.

Luke 7:39 states that the Pharisees said among themselves, "*This man, if he were a prophet, would have known who and what manner of woman this is that toucheth him: for she is a sinner.*"

Jesus appeared to ignore the men's little chitter-chatter and murmuring; however, in the following verses, Jesus tried to open their blind eyes by telling them a parable. Jesus asked Simon to answer a question in the form of a parable: *"There was a certain creditor, which had two debtors: the one owed five hundred pence, and the other fifty. And when they had nothing to pay, he frankly forgave them both. Tell me therefore, which of them will love him most?"*

In Luke 7:43: *Simon answered and said, "I suppose that he, to whom he forgave most."* Jesus answered by saying , *"Thou hast rightly judged."* (Meaning that Simon gave Him the right answer.)

And before Jesus left, he turned to the humble woman (prostitute) and said, *"Seest thou this woman? I entered into thine house, thou gavest me no water for my feet: but she hath washed my feet with tears, and wiped them with the hairs of her head. Thou gavest me no kiss: but this woman since the time I came in hath not ceased to kiss my feet. My head with oil thou didst not anoint: but this woman hath anointed my feet with ointment. Wherefore, I say unto thee, Her sins, which are many, are forgiven: for she loved much: but to whom little is forgiven, the same loveth little."*

Luke 7:48: Jesus says to her, *"Thy sins are forgiven."*

Luke 7:50: Jesus says to the woman, *"Thy faith hath saved thee; go in peace."*

Glory to God! The woman who was judged harshly by men was blessed by Jesus! He forgave her of all her sins.

Again, Jesus says today, *"Go in peace!"*

Just keep on loving Jesus with all your heart! All your sins have been forgiven! All your sins have been washed away! You have a clean slate!

Let us all want to wash Jesus' feet with our tears because He loves us so much, more than we will ever know, and He washes away all our sins.

# Woman at the Well

## John 4:7-26

John 4:7 says, *"There cometh a woman of Samaria to draw water"* [from Jacob's well...]

The woman was from the village of Sychar which was a few miles southeast of the city of Samaria and fairly close to Mount Gerizim as well as to the ground given by Jacob to Joseph. Since the village of Sychar had water, it is possible that the woman's solitary journey to Jacob's Well from day to day indicates a species of ostracism by the other women of the community.

Jesus broke the silence with a request for a drink. It was a natural request in view of His weariness. It is a poignant reminder of our Lord's humanity here on earth. The departure of the disciples was providential, for the woman would not have entered into discussion with Jesus in their presence. Two things amazed the woman: That Jesus would make such a request of a *woman*, for a Rabbi avoided contact with *women in public*; and particularly that He would speak to one who was a Samaritan. Jesus did not make "common use" with Samaritans. It is made clear that Jews had no dealings with Samaritans.

John 4:7 states that Jesus said to the Samaritan woman, *"Give me to drink."*

(The disciples were gone away unto the city to buy meat.)

John 4:9 states that the Samaritan woman replied, *"How is it that thou, being a Jew, askest drink of me, which am a woman of Samaria? For the Jews have no dealings with the Samaritans."*

In reply, Jesus moved away from His own need to suggest that the woman had a greater need, a need that He was able to supply through the gift of God. Jesus, who was always able to use analogies and metaphors perfectly, used the physical water in the well to represent spiritual or "living water."

Thinking in terms of the physical well beneath them, the woman was puzzled, because Jesus did not bring a container for drawing water, and the well was deep. At the bottom of the deep well, there was living (running) water fed by a spring.

**"Could this Rabbi hope to conjure up what Jacob was only able to secure by hard toil? He would indeed be greater if He could do this," she thought.**

Jesus explained to the woman that the physical water from the well had to be drawn by toil and consumed over and over again, but the water He (Christ) dispenses will quench her thirst forever; it will give everlasting life!

A parallel may be drawn with the repeated sacrifices of God's children in the old covenant in comparison to the perfect, one-time sacrifice of the perfect Lamb, Jesus, who represents "living water."

Still not fully understanding Jesus, the woman asked for the water that her lot might be easier. However, before the woman could receive the gift of living water she had to realize how desperately she needed it. The gift was for the inner life (inner spirit) which, in her case, was desperately in need of healing and filling.

Jesus told her about her marital status, only to prove that He is the Savior and wanted to gain her faith so that He could help her. Jesus didn't do it to humiliate or hurt her. Also, Jesus was discreet when talking to her; they were alone. No one else was around.

The dreary history of her marital life was unfolded by Jesus and by her own admission.

To the woman, Jesus was first thought of as a Jew; then, she gave him the title "Sir," and she (finally) called him a prophet. He had looked into her soul. Now, the woman was "heart-hungry" to know the way of God!

Regardless of what you've done, you can become "heart-hungry" for Jesus, and He will give you "living water" that never runs dry!

# The Woman Taken in Adultery

Luke 2:46 states that as a child, Jesus visited the Temple to be taught.

In John 8:3-4 Jesus as a man was again in the Temple—not to be taught but to teach. With people crowding around Him, the teaching session was interrupted by the arrival of scribes and Pharisees who were leading a woman whom they said was caught in the "very act" of adultery. Angered at Jesus' success and frustrated by their inability to get rid of Him, these leaders now seized an opportunity to embarrass Jesus in the midst of all the people watching. Of course, they also embarrassed the woman by placing her in the midst.

John 8:4-5 states that the scribes and Pharisees said unto Jesus, *"Master, this woman was taken in adultery, in the very act. Now Moses in the law commanded us, that such should be stoned: but what sayest thou?"*

Reminding Jesus of the requirement of stoning for this offense (Deut. 22:23-24), these leaders sought His verdict on the matter. They were tempting Him by putting Him in a dilemma. If He upheld the law, which was apparently not being applied rigorously in such cases (mostly only used when convenient), He could be made to appear heartless.

If He advocated mercy, He could be heralded as having too lenient a view for the application of the law. (Remember, before Jesus' birth, the laws were what people understood.) However, if the Pharisees were genuinely concerned about any laws at all, they would have brought the male offender also to be stoned or judged.

Where was the man? Maybe the woman was innocent, and they didn't catch her in the very act of adultery as they claimed happened. Why would a woman alone be stoned for committing adultery. Adultery is a three-fold matter. Someone has to be married, and someone has to commit the act of having "sex with someone outside of their marriage."

Where are the other two people who had connections with this woman, the two people who could testify on her behalf or the two people who can testify against her.

The whole matter was a mockery, anyway. It was all a ridiculous act by the leaders.

We learn in John 8:7 that Jesus, however, shifted the attention from himself and the woman to the accusers by saying to her accusers, *"He that is without sin among you, let him first cast a stone."*

And in John 8:10-11 Jesus asked, *"Woman, where are those thine accusers? hath no man condemned thee?"* She answered, *"No man, Lord."* Jesus said, *"Neither do I condemn thee: go, and sin no more."*

Jesus was saying to her as He says to everyone today, *"You have a clean slate; go and sin no more!"*

# From the Master's Table

Matthew 15:21-28 and Mark 7:24-30 tells the story about a woman's faith and hope:

A girl had been tormented by a demon. The Bible does not say if this tormenting resulted in physical or emotional problems. However, her mother believed the girl could be healed. The mother approached Jesus, showing great faith, and the daughter was healed.

> *Jesus left that place and went away to the district of Tyre and Sidon. Just then a Canannite woman from that region came out and started shouting, "Have mercy on me, Lord, Son of David; my daughter is tormented by a demon." But he did not answer her at all. And his disciples came and urged him, saying, "Send her away, for she keeps shouting after us." He answered, "I was sent only to the lost sheep of the house of Israel." But she came and knelt before him saying, "Lord, help me." He answered, "It is not fair to take the children's food and throw it to the dogs." She said, "Yes, Lord, yet even the dogs eat the crumbs that fall from their master's table." Then Jesus answered her, "Woman, great is your faith! Let it be done for you as you wish." And her daughter was healed instantly.*

Please pray, first. Then, read these scriptures from the Bible:

JOHN 8:7

*"He that is without sin among you, let him first cast a stone."*

PSALM 27:10

*"When my father and my mother forsake me, then the Lord will take me up."*

ROMANS 3:23

*"For all have sinned, and come short of the glory of God."*

2 CORINTHIANS 5:17

*"If any man be in Christ, he is a new creature: Old things are passed away; behold all things become new."*

ROMANS 8:1

*"There is therefore now no condemnation to them which are in Christ Jesus, who walk not after the flesh, but after the Spirit."*

Remember: Nothing is too hard for God! Now, go in peace and be whole of thy plague!

I say to all the women who are suffering: If you can't find Jesus standing up, fall down! Throw yourself at your Master's feet! Man might not understand why you are shouting and begging for forgiveness. Man might not understand why you are crying out to the Lord whom you believe is the Savior, Jesus Christ! Man might judge you, call you names, and tell you to go home, but don't leave! Jesus will recognize your great faith! It is time for you to walk in your divine destiny!

# SECTION III

## Your Turn to Live Out Your Divine Purpose

# Letter from God to Women

When I created the heavens and the earth, I spoke
them into being. When I created man, I formed
him and breathed life into his nostrils.

But you, woman, I fashioned after I breathed the breath
of life into man because your nostrils are too delicate.
I allowed a deep sleep to come over man so I could patiently
and perfectly fashion you, woman. Man was put to sleep
so that he could not interfere with the creativity.

From one bone, I fashioned you. I chose the bone that
protects man's life. I chose the rib, which protects his
heart and lungs and supports him, as you are meant
to do. Around this one bone, I shaped you,
I modeled you, my beautiful lady.

I created you perfectly and beautifully. Your characteristics
are as the rib, strong yet delicate and fragile. You
provide protection for the most delicate organ in man,
his heart. His heart is the center of his being;

his lungs hold the breath of life. The ribcage will allow itself to be broken before it will allow damage to the heart. Support man as the ribcage supports the body, because without you, man has no hope, no life.

You were not taken from his feet, to be under him, nor were you taken from his head, to be above him. You were taken from his side, to stand beside him and be held close to his side.

You are my perfect angel…You are and will always be my beautiful little girl. You have grown to be a splendid woman of excellence, and my eyes fill when I see the virtues in your heart. Your eyes…don't change them. Your eyes are the eyes of compassion.

Your lips are the lips of truth. Your voice is the voice of kindness. Your heart is the heart of love; I call you my sweet charity. Your graceful hands are so gentle to touch, and from your womb, you bear the ultimate fruit; life is born from your womb! My beautiful life-giver, I've caressed your sweet face in your deepest sleep. I've held your heart close to mine. I love to watch you, my Divine. You are my Psalm. You are never old, but you, like fine wine, get sweeter with time.

Of all that lives and breathes, you are most like me. Hold your head up high, and please don't cast your pearls to swine. Give me your praise; yes, don't ever stop praising me! I've given you special discernment and special intuition. If man leaves you alone, I'll still be by your side. I'll never leave you!

Adam walked with me in the cool of the day, yet he was lonely; he could not see me or touch me. He could only feel me. So everything I wanted Adam to share and experience with me, I fashioned in you; my beautiful, special woman, because you are an extension of me. Whoso findeth a wife findeth a good thing, and obtaineth favour of the Lord.

Man represents my image, woman my emotions, even my thoughts. Together, your spirit and man's spirit represent the totality of God.
*Oh, great woman of God, my beautiful bride, I love you!*

So men, treat women well. Love her; respect her, for she is fragile; however, without her, you are nothing, because she is that perfect extension of you. Share this with all the women you know, so that they may always remember how special they are. God loves all of you, women. You are God's wonderful creation!

# Your Purpose

As you learn to walk in your divine purpose, God will bless you with people who will help you find the way. He will also place in your life people who will draw strength from you because of the experiences you've lived.

List the names and telephone numbers of people who support you and those you are blessed to support.

_____     _____

_____     _____

_____     _____

_____     _____

_____     _____

Without a vision, the people perish. Outline your purpose and your family's purpose in God, by creating a "mission statement." This statement can be personal or it can be written for your whole family. Write your mission statement, memorize it, and repeat it over and over until it is embedded in your spirit. Allow it to become a part of your daily life.

My Personal Mission Statement

_____

_____

_____

_____

Our Family's Mission Statement

_____

_____

_____

_____

My Personal Prayer

_____

_____

_____

_____

## YOUR PRAYERS

### *Prayer for Inner Healing and Closeness to God*

Heavenly Father, I bow in worship and praise before
you and cover myself with the blood of Jesus Christ.
I claim the protection over myself and over all
my family members and other loved ones.
I thank you God, for your Son Jesus,
who died on the cross not only for my sins

but also for the sins of the whole world.
I thank you, Jesus, because you are the same
yesterday, today, and forever.

Lord, I have suffered some horrible hurts and pain.
Please heal me and make me whole; help me to forgive
those who have hurt me. I know that you will give me
the strength to forgive them, and I thank you.

I forgive _____

I forgive _____

I forgive _____

I forgive _____

I forgive _____

As I forgive others, please Lord, forgive me.
I am sorry for hurting you. You deserve the best,
and I want to learn to love you the right way.
I don't want to hurt you or grieve your Spirit
anymore, and I know that you know my heart.
You are so beautiful; you are the one and only
God, and you deserve the best from me.
I want to do better, and I am going to praise
and worship you this day.

I thank you, Jesus, for waking me up this morning.
You didn't have to do it, but you did! Bless you,
oh Lord; you are my hero. When I can't talk
to anyone else, I can always call on you and talk
to you. I don't want to keep anything from you.
I want to share everything with you.
Everything in my life belongs to you anyway,
and I dedicate all I have to you, all my gifts
and talents belong to you.

I don't have to worry, because even while
I'm on my knees, you are taking away my hurts
and filling my voids. As I pray to you, you are
taking away my fears, the fear of rejection

and fear of failure. You're also taking away guilt; because of you, there is no condemnation in my soul.

Jesus, you knew all about me even before I was born. You were there with me when I was born, and you love me and have a wonderful plan for my life. You died so that I could be set free. Please help me to walk in the right way to fulfill the destiny you have planned for me. Lord, help me to be more like you. Mold me into your image, into your likeness.

Today is your day, and I'm going to bless you with praise and prayers. I will not complain, worry, fear, or be selfish today. I am going to proclaim your love to everyone around me by the way I live my life today. I want to please you, Lord, and I don't want to grieve your Spirit today. Help me to keep my eyes stayed on you. You are omnipotent, omnipresent, and omniscient. You are God, and there is no other! Amen.

# Prayer of Divine Purpose
## (A Spiritual Warfare Prayer)

If you desire a closer relationship with God, you must pray. The Bible says that we are to "pray without ceasing," and there is a kind of prayer that gives you the strength to defeat the devil, stand up in the authority given to us by Christ Jesus, and retake all the blessings that God has given to us and to our family.

This kind of prayer is called *"A Spiritual Warfare Prayer,"* or it is what the early Friends called "The Lamb's War." Christians have always believed that the real war is spiritual, not physical.

Christians believe that we battle *"...not against flesh and blood, but against principalities, against powers, against the rulers of the darkness of this world, against spiritual wickedness in high places."* (Eph. 6:12).

Dear Heavenly Father,
I bow in worship and praise before you.
I cover myself with the blood of Jesus Christ

and claim the protection of the blood for my
family, our home, our spirits, souls, and bodies.

I surrender myself completely in every area
of my life to you. I take a stand against
all the workings of the devil that would try and
hinder me and my family from best serving you.

I address myself to the true and Living God.
I am God's child. I resist the devil. No weapon formed
against me shall prosper. I put on the whole armor
of God. I take authority over this day, in Jesus'
Name. Let it be prosperous in every way
for me, and let me walk in your love, Lord.
In the name of Jesus, I loose the spirit of healing,
health, prosperity, and spirituality.

The Holy Spirit leads and guides me today.
In my life today, I destroy and tear down
all the strongholds of satan and smash
the plans of satan that have been formed
against me and my family. I tear down the
strongholds of the enemy against my mind,
and I surrender my mind and heart
to you, Blessed Holy Spirit.

*I forgive everyone who has hurt me.*
*I realize that I cannot be forgiven unless*
*I forgive others. I lovingly forgive others*
*as my Lord and Savior forgives me.*

I affirm, Heavenly Father, that you
have not given me the spirit of fear, but power
and love in the name of Jesus, the Son of the Living
God; and I refuse to fear, refuse to doubt, refuse
to worry, because I have authority (power) over all
the forces of the enemy, and nothing shall by any
means hurt me (Luke 10:19). I claim complete
and absolute victory over the forces of darkness
in the name of Jesus, and I bind the enemy
and command him to loose my peace, joy,

prosperity, and every member of my family
for the glory of God and by faith. I call it
done today in the name of Jesus!

I claim a hedge of protection around myself,
my spouse, and my children (insert names)
throughout this day and night. I ask you, God,
in the name of Jesus, to dispatch angels
to surround my spouse, my children, and me
today, and to put them throughout our house,
around our cars, souls, and bodies. I ask angels
to protect my house from an intrusion and
to protect me and my family from any harmful
demonic physical or mental attacks.
I ask this prayer in the name of Jesus.

Thank you, God, in the name of Jesus.
Amen.

# Your Future

As I wrote in the beginning of this book—*I want you to know that* **you can be set free!** After reading the stories about other women, I hope that you realize that you are not alone. Although you might have been filled with resentment, anger, depression, or with overwhelming guilt and shame, now you know that you are not the only one who has suffered. You know now that you are not being punished by God, and that your sin isn't any greater than the sins of others.

Sin is sin and God sent Jesus as the solution.

Oh great woman of God, continue to love Him in your prayers—know that God has been waiting for you and loving you since the beginning of time. God has a wonderful plan for your life! The door is open; the way is made! There is going to be a great move of God like never before, and you will be a part of it. Expect God's revelation and His glory over your life.

*It's time for you to live with a purpose and to walk into your divine destiny!*

# Conclusion

I feel like I just birthed a baby. This book is a dream come true for me; not because of any material gain, but because for as long as I can remember, I've wanted to use my pain to help others. To God be the glory! It's beautiful just to think that people, many of whom I'll never physically meet, will be healed and will find hope from reading this book.

If this book has encouraged you, please share it with the other women in your life. I hope and pray that you receive healing and prosperity (spiritually and physically). You can read over the stories and Bible verses again and again. If you know someone who is in pain, share with them the stories and Scripture readings that helped you to find peace and hope.

I want all women to know that they can be "set free!" Woman of divine destiny, you're not suffering alone. There are many women just like you, and they want to hear your testimony! Nothing happens by chance. God has a special purpose for your life. The things that we "go through" are not only for us; we endure and suffer to help others.

No matter what happens in your life (even during the most painful time), please remember that "God is in control!" Regardless of how bad things look in the beginning (or right now), God will take care of you, because there is nothing too hard for God!

God loves you, and He wants you to walk in your divine destiny!

*A portion of the proceeds received from the sale of this book will be donated to organizations that help abused women and children.*